The Right
Pastor

Seeking God's Man
for Your Church

Wesley E. Johnson

REGULAR BAPTIST PRESS
1300 North Meacham Road
Schaumburg, Illinois 60173-4806

THE RIGHT PASTOR: SEEKING GOD'S MAN FOR YOUR CHURCH
(A Manual for the Pastoral Search Committee)
This edition adapted for use in fundamental Baptist churches.

© 1985, 1989 by Wesley E. Johnson
as *Pastoral Search Book*

First printing   1987
Second printing   1989
Third printing   1990
Fourth printing   1994
Fifth printing   1995
Sixth printing   1997
RBP printing   1999 (by permission from author)

Each member of the pastoral search committee should have a copy of this manual.
Permission is hereby granted to the pastoral search committee of a congregation to reproduce the surveys and forms necessary in its efforts to find a pastor.

Regular Baptist Press
Schaumburg, Illinois
1-800-727-4440
Printed in U.S.A.
All rights reserved.
ISBN 0-87227-205-2

Contents

INDEX OF ITEMS

Foreword

VIRTUALLY EVERY WEEK churches ask me to submit names of possible pastoral candidates. The process of trying to match prospective pastors with appropriate churches can be frustrating. Customarily I will include disclaimers in my replies to emphasize that my recommendations are not guaranteed. I advise the search committees and the churches to conduct careful evaluations to determine the worthiness of the men.

The task of evaluating the suitability of potential candidates is no small assignment. The work would be easier if I, like a denominational bishop, had the authority to place pastors in churches. However, this approach does not match our Baptist polity, nor would I want that responsibility. The local church has the duty of facilitating the pastoral search process.

Most pastoral search committees do not view themselves as qualified for the task. They readily admit their inadequacies and ask for help. For some time I have wanted to provide a step-by-step guide for churches that would lead them through the unfamiliar territory of finding a pastor.

What a delight to discover a most helpful tool! *The Right Pastor* is a practical and easy-to-use workbook that will lead a church through the process of pastoral search from start to finish. Wesley Johnson has done a masterful job of "covering all the bases."

Wesley graciously permitted Regular Baptist Press to edit his manuscript to suit an independent Baptist model. I am confident that any church that follows these guidelines will find the challenge far easier. This workbook will point the church's pastoral search process in the right direction.

John Greening
GARBC National Representative
Schaumburg, Illinois

Introduction

ANY LOCAL CHURCH has episodes in its history that may alter both its life and its future. One such event is a change in pastoral leadership. Because of the position and influence of the pastor within a congregation, the calling of a man to shepherd the flock becomes an all-important decision.

The purpose of this manual is to help a church, through an orderly process, find a properly qualified and gifted pastor. I do not guarantee that this manual will ensure the perfect union of a pastor and a congregation, but I believe it can prevent a tragic union.

People make decisions in response to both objective as well as subjective information. The material in this manual is designed to help a church obtain objective information in its decision-making process. The profile developed will provide a framework by which both the committee and the congregation can view and evaluate a candidate. The material will also give structure to the process.

This manual was produced for churches holding the congregational form of church government. Because God's Holy Spirit indwells each Christian, I also believe the consensus of the congregation expressed by its vote affirms the calling of a candidate.

The manual has been used in approximately a thousand churches, whose memberships have ranged from twenty members to more than two thousand members.

May the Lord guide and bless your congregation at this important time in the ongoing history of your church.

CHAPTER 1

The Establishment of the Pastoral Search Committee

The Importance of the Pastoral Search Committee

The success, effectiveness, and tenure of the pastoral ministry is directly related to the work of a pastoral search committee. The quest of a thoughtful Christian is to know the will of God for his/her own life. Likewise, the quest of a pastoral search committee is to help the congregation and pastoral candidate understand and determine God's will. To do this, the committee must establish the needs, expectations, and goals of the church and also decide what gifts and qualities a candidate must have to meet them. Failing to make this evaluation will send the church into a cyclical process of changing pastors and thus will dilute the effectiveness of the church's ministry.

The Selection of the Pastoral Search Committee

It is best when the church constitution directs the congregation on how the selection of the pastoral search committee should take place. This direction will usually give the congregation a neutral profile of the pastoral search committee, particularly if the last pastor left under pressure. If no constitutional directives exist, a special congregational meeting must be called for the explicit purpose of estab-

lishing the pastoral search committee. The method of nomination, the size of the committee, and the required vote should be defined before any specific names are brought to the floor of the business meeting. The committee should be elected by the entire church membership.

The committee should be established soon after the pastor resigns. Some members will feel uneasy about taking such action before the pastor leaves, but the issue of the committee must quickly be addressed, as the calling process will take from four to twenty-four months.

The committee will function best with five to seven members. It should not exceed nine members and should have an odd number.

In the event that there are no constitutional directives, the following is a suggested procedure for nominating members to the committee: (1) Ask the members of the congregation to list on a ballot their choices for the pastoral search committee. The number listed by each member should not exceed the number to serve on the committee. (2) The names receiving the most votes are then put on a ballot. This list would contain twice the number required. (3) Then the church will elect the committee from those so nominated.

The Qualifications
of the Pastoral Search Committee

Members of the committee should meet the following qualifications. Each one should be

1. An active member of the local congregation;

2. Known for prayer and spiritual maturity;

3. Respected by the congregation;

4. Self-committed to the time and energy necessary to complete the task;

5. Representative. Members collectively should represent the full spectrum of the congregation.

The Organization
of the Pastoral Search Committee

Unless the chairman of the committee has been designated by the church, it is well to have the chairman of the church/deacon board convene the first meeting. At this meeting the following officers should be selected.

Chairman

The chairman must possess qualities of leadership, a sensitive spirit, and an ability to get things done. He should make available a prepared agenda for each member for each meeting, chair all meetings, expedite and/or delegate all activities of the committee, and be the official voice of the committee.

Vice Chairman

The vice chairman will act in the absence of the chairman or on instruction of the committee.

Secretary

The secretary will keep an accurate record of all committee proceedings, provide copies of minutes for each committee member, notify members of scheduled meetings, and carry on correspondence as directed. All minutes and correspondence must be kept strictly confidential.

The flow chart (Item E, p. 43), timeline schedule (Item A, p. 25), and this manual should be explained and adopted by the committee as a guideline to its functioning. Each member should have a copy of this manual.

The Responsibilities
of the Pastoral Search Committee

At the same meeting during which the committee is selected, the congregation should also spell out in writing the job description and expectations it has for the pastoral search committee. The following is a list of what should be considered.

1. Is the pastoral search committee responsible for obtaining pulpit supply and/or an interim pastor?

2. Is the committee responsible for all aspects of the calling process? Examples:
   a. Establishing qualifications
   b. Screening possible candidates
   c. Presenting the candidate
   d. Arranging candidate exposure and time at church
   e. Negotiating a financial package
   f. Handling business sessions
   g. Writing a letter of "call"
   h. Arranging the move

3. What type of budget will the pastoral search committee be allotted?
   a. Telephone
   b. Mailing
   c. Travel for committee members to interview possible candidates
   d. Expenses for candidate

4. Concerning negotiations with the candidate, in what areas is the committee

empowered to speak and work?

a. Salary
b. Housing
c. Utilities
d. Moving expenses
e. Car expenses
f. Hospitalization
g. Retirement
h. Conference time and expenses
i. Vacation
j. Personal ministry days
k. Continuing education
l. Book allowance
m. Professional allowance
n. Miscellaneous

The Relationship of the Pastoral Search Committee to Leaders in an Association of Churches

It is helpful for a pastoral search committee to contact a proper leader if the church is a part of a fellowship or association. In the General Association of Regular Baptist Churches (GARBC), for example, the state representative and the national representative have a vested interest in helping to secure the best possible pastor for the church. Experience has shown that the advice and help a state or national representative can give often saves the committee from costly and time-consuming errors.

The Interrelationship of the Members of the Pastoral Search Committee

As in any joint effort, people do not become a team merely by being appointed to some committee. They may be members of the same committee, but until they know and trust each other enough to exercise risks, they will have difficulty in accomplishing their assigned task. This is particularly true if the church has suffered some difficulty with the previous pastor. The pastoral search committee has been placed in the position of *union* by appointment. The pastoral search committee must develop a relationship of *unity* by commitment.

This relationship involves taking quality time to know and build mutual confidence in each other. Therefore, at the first meeting the priority must be to spend time in sharing concerns, studying a portion of God's Word, and prayer. These items should be included in the agenda of every meeting. Oneness of spirit and consensus of opinion cannot be obtained if there is a fracture in personal unity.

CHAPTER 2

The Procedure for the Pastoral Search Committee

The Pastoral Search Committee and Communication with the Congregation

When a pastor leaves, people typically speculate as to the reasons for his move. Unless these reasons are clear, an undercurrent of strange rumors often arises. Rumors tend to polarize people and activate needless tensions. These feelings of tension are difficult to isolate and resolve. As a result, the pastoral search committee comes into its role under an atmosphere of suspicion. Two notions arise: "They are not really doing their job, or else we would know more by now," and "We are being railroaded into this."

Another issue the pastoral search committee must face is the matter of ownership. The committee can be excited about a certain candidate, but how will the congregation respond? Ownership of the process, as well as of the candidate, must be generated among the total congregation.

The one great factor for both the establishment of ownership and the stifling of criticism is communication. All meetings of the pastoral search committee should be announced. Every meeting should be reported by a sentence or two in the Sunday bulletin as to actions or decisions.

Names of candidates should not be revealed to anyone outside the committee until such a candidate has agreed by a written commitment that he will be at your church on a specific weekend to candidate. It is a good idea, if possible, to bring a man to the church as a "pulpit supply" initially. Then the committee can better evaluate him and decide whether to go to the next step: candidacy. Keeping names concealed is especially true of a simple list of suggested names. A pastor may not know you are considering his name, and he may have no interest. Yet a church's interest in the man could easily creep back to his own church, consequently putting him in an embarrassing situation.

The Pastoral Search Committee and the Interim Pastor

The consideration of an interim pastor is especially important at this juncture in the church's ministry. If the pastoral search committee is not responsible for the engaging of an interim pastor, the following information should be channeled to the proper place.

Consider these seven common questions:
1. **When is it advisable to engage an interim pastor?**
   - When the previous pastor left under pressure, the interim's tenure will

provide a period of healing and restoration.

- When the church does not have adequate lay leadership, the interim's leadership will be a rallying point for the congregation and can initiate positive actions and feelings.
- When there is division and polarization within the congregation, the interim can give objective spiritual leadership from a neutral platform.
- When the church needs a transitional process, the interim has more liberty to deal head-on with such issues, since he does not represent some vested interest group.

2. **When is an interim pastor not really needed?**

- When the lay leadership is strong and capable of taking up many of the normal everyday responsibilities of the pastor. The one issue here is the availability of time. If those leaders, because of lack of time and the size of the church, will be unable to cover the work, they should consider an interim pastor.
- When supply preachers are readily available.
- When the church is healthy and there are no dividing factions.

3. **What provisions should be made for an interim pastor?**

- He should be paid commensurate with the time he is asked to give to the church.
- He should be provided housing if he is expected to stay in the community. This provision should also include related benefits.
- He should be paid for every week and Sunday he has been contracted to serve. If a pastoral candidate is presented on a weekend, the interim pastor should still be paid. Only when the pastor comes should the contract be broken.

4. **What should be the tenure of an interim pastor?**

- The usual tenure is three months. That term is shortened only by the call and presence of a new pastor.
- No interim should serve for more than four terms, or twelve months. His effectiveness diminishes rapidly after twelve months. If the people really enjoy him, the pastoral search committee has a tendency to procrastinate.

5. **What understanding should a church have with an interim pastor?**

- Before he comes, he and the church should clearly understand his tenure.
- He should be informed that your church will not consider him as a candidate. If pressure arises from within the church to have him as a candidate and he so desires, he must resign as the interim. He will be put through the same process as all other candidates; and if he is not considered or does not receive the call, he can no longer be the interim.
- He cannot serve on the pastoral search committee.
- He should not be present during the days a candidate is presented, except for funerals and emergencies.

6. **How does a church find men to serve as interim pastors?**

- In the GARBC, the state representatives or the national representative in the Ministry Resource Center in Schaumburg, Illinois, will usually have the names of several available men.

7. How is the interim pastor called?

- Because the interim pastor is called for a limited term, the pastoral search committee and/or the church board are usually authorized to call the interim.
- If the church desires or requires that an interim be called by a vote of the congregation, it should be by a simple majority vote. The reason is that a church usually needs an interim when it has experienced problems. It is both difficult and sometimes detrimental to force a body for a unanimous vote concerning an interim pastor.

The Pastoral Search Committee and the Development of a Church and Pastoral Profile

Before any names are discussed in the committee, the committee must develop a pastoral profile. Your committee will receive many names of "favorite sons" (candidates suggested by the congregation) and résumés from men looking for a church. All names should be recorded but not presented for discussion. Any name brought up tends to destroy the ability of the committee to be objective in the research for a profile.

To develop a pastoral profile, the committee must research and evaluate the church's needs and expectations. In the process of determining the present needs of the church, be careful that the committee does not make its evaluation on either the weaknesses or strengths of the previous pastor.

In determining needs, do not begin by asking the committee members what they would like to see in a new man. The friends of the previous pastor will list his strengths as needs, and the "not-so-friendly" will list

the needs in terms of his weaknesses. It is more than probable that both sides will miss the real issues and needs of the church. Besides blinding the committee, this approach can develop parties within the committee. It will also be important for the committee to look at future needs and goals.

It has been observed that the committee that does its homework will have an easier time throughout the whole transitional period. The members will always know the kind of person they need, and consequently they will move more quickly and with greater confidence. When the work of the committee is done well, the pastor's tenure will likely be longer.

This process has five phases. Note the timeline schedule for these phases (see Item A, page 25).

PHASE ONE—Acquisition of Church Information (Item B, p. 27)

The committee must gather and know the general facts about the church. The facts will not only aid the search committee but will also be used in communication with the candidates.

PHASE TWO—Acquisition of Church Goals

The church board should enumerate the goals and expectations of the church for the next three, five, and ten years. The board members should spell out what they expect and hope to be as a church by those dates. They should include items such as membership, attendance, general budget, missions budget, church programs, outreach, church expansion, church planting, and building programs. The board members should also make available the church's mission statement and should spell out what they see as the church's priorities and vision for the coming years. A state and/or national representative or associational leader can provide advice and encouragement in these areas.

PHASE THREE—Acquisition of Pastoral History (Item C, p. 31)

The church should compile a pastoral history of the church. This will enlighten the committee concerning any recurring issues that have possibly been overlooked in the calling processes of the past. This is also a place to consider the expectations and job description for the pastor (Item T, p. 111).

PHASE FOUR—Congregational Survey (Items D₁ and D₂, pp. 33, 39)

The committee must survey the congregation as to its expectations for a pastor. To obtain the greatest return, survey forms should be distributed at a morning worship service. Allow about ten to twelve minutes to complete them; then collect them immediately. Survey forms can be mailed, but the result is not great in this way—usually only about 30 percent of a mailing finds its way back.

Because congregational ownership of both the process and pastoral candidate is so important, many churches will also conduct personal surveys of groups of people within the congregation, such as Sunday School classes, fellowship groups, youth groups, senior citizens, and so on. In these sessions, members of the search committee will spend at least an hour with the group. A member from the committee will moderate the sessions, and another will take notes. The following is a possible list of subjects presented:

- Biblical admonition, such as the value of searching for wisdom (Proverbs 2; Psalm 139:2, 3; 1 Corinthians 2:10)

- The pastoral search process
- Expectations concerning the new pastor
- Suggestions of possible new programs or emphases
- Concerns the members have for their group
- Concerns they have for the church
- The strengths they see in the church
- The weaknesses they see in the church

PHASE FIVE—Profile Development

Upon receipt of all the material, the committee is then ready to compile a profile of the prospective pastor. Carefully categorize and integrate the material so that you can list in the pastor's profile the qualities you believe you need. After you have made the list, put the qualities in a priority order and check those items that must be found in the pastor. Remember, the profile cannot be perfectly matched with a man, but now at least you have explicit guidelines with which to work and compare.

After the statistical profile has been established, a committee member should be assigned to put the profile into prose form. This form should be mailed to the members of the congregation, and this communication will help the congregation in the matter of ownership. It will also help to solidify the thinking and begin to give unity in the process of deciding upon a specific candidate.

The Pastoral Search Committee and the Calling Procedure

Please note the flow chart (Item E, p. 43) and timeline (Item A, p. 25).

STEP ONE—The Acquisition of Names and Résumés of Potential Candidates

Your pastoral profile should be mailed to the national representative and/or state representatives, who will be able to send you a number of résumés. You will also receive names from other sources, such as seminaries and members of your church. *Do not allow friendships to cause you to bypass the pastoral profile.* Always use it as your frame of reference.

STEP TWO—Review of all potential candidates

Carefully review all names of potential candidates. If, within the committee, a name is found to be unacceptable, seek the reasons but don't argue. Then simply set that name aside. If a candidate is unacceptable at this level, he probably never will be acceptable.

To a candidate who is acceptable, send a letter to determine his interest. You will find a sample copy of such a letter (Item F, p. 47). You will notice that the request is non-committal. The purpose is to allow both the committee and the pastor to proceed without obligation to each other. (The average positive response is less than 50 percent.) If you do not have a résumé of the candidate, you should send a pastoral questionnaire (Items G_1 and G_2, pp. 49, 55).

At this point you may wish to send informative material concerning the church and the community. A suggested list of information can be found on Item H (p. 71). The committee may decide to wait with this material until Step Four. It is advisable to fill out a form for each candidate so that you will always know where you are in the process of his candidacy (Item S, p. 109).

STEP THREE—The verification of responses

After you receive an affirmative response from a candidate, write immediately to notify him that you have received his material. *Do not fail to write* to each of the references that he has given to you (Item I, p. 73). To the candidate who responded negatively, reply with a note of thanks.

STEP FOUR—The screening of possible candidates

After you have received all material concerning the candidates, review it in light of your pastoral profile. If a candidate is unacceptable, send him a letter immediately. Select several candidates who best fulfill your profile, then set up an appointment for an interview. If a candidate is close enough to visit, set up the appointment in some neutral place away from his city. If a candidate is a distance away, a conference phone call should be arranged.

A suggested procedure and list of questions is given on Item J (p. 79). If you have not given him the material concerning your church and committee in Step Two, be sure each candidate you interviewed has the material in his hands before your appointment with him.

STEP FIVE—The evaluation of the candidate

To more objectively evaluate the candidate, you may wish to use part of the Evaluation Worksheet as given in Item Q_1 (p. 97). If no candidates are acceptable, you will return to those candidates not yet interviewed in Step Four. If no names are left, you will return to Step One. If a candidate is unacceptable, please write him immediately of your decision. From those candidates whom you find acceptable, proceed to Step Six.

STEP SIX—The evaluation of the candidate's preaching performance

If at all possible you will want to visit each candidate in his church to hear him preach. If this is prohibitive because of cost, you should ask for an audiotape or a videotape. Before traveling to a church, make sure your candidate is preaching. Try not to be conspicuous in the service, and do not announce the purpose of the visit to anyone in the congregation. If you have more than four people, do not sit together.

STEP SEVEN—The choice of several prime candidates

After you have evaluated their preaching style and ability and you have several potential candidates, or one candidate, proceed to Step Eight. (You may use Items Q_{1-6} at this point. See pages 97—102.) Notify those candidates who are no longer potential candidates and would not be considered if the church rejects the prime candidate.

STEP EIGHT—The selection of one prime candidate

This is the most difficult step, especially if you have more than two candidates to consider. This is the point where the committee must rank each candidate and make its priority choice. (You may use Items Q_2 and Q_3 at this point. See pages 98, 99, 101, and 102.) The pastoral search committee should be unanimous on the candidate. If it happens that the committee members have not visited their number-one candidate in his church, they should do so now. It is imperative that the congregation be presented with one candidate. To present more than one at a time turns the process into a popularity contest. You are not hiring a preacher, you are calling a pastor/shepherd. Allow God's Holy Spirit to work in your people by making one choice at a time. To present two candidates will always divide

the congregation into "your candidate" and "my candidate." Set a date for the candidate to visit your church. A suggested schedule for a candidating visit is found in Item L (p. 87). Publish and present the material concerning the candidate to the congregation at least ten days before his scheduled visit.

STEP NINE—The church board's support and the pastor's remuneration/other benefits (Items K and N, pp. 83, 91)

If negotiations with the church and candidate concerning his remuneration, his benefits, and any other arrangements have not been completed, they should be agreed upon and put into writing at this point. A schedule for candidating should be set and agreed upon by the board. Other items that need to be considered are vacation time (schedule for years of service), continuing education, Sundays for ministry, conferences, and form of remuneration (Item T, p. 111).

STEP TEN—The congregational approval and call

A congregational meeting to vote on the call should be set for the week following the visit of the candidate. It is well to give the members at least a week to pray and think over their decision. Unless the voting is clearly defined in the constitution, you need to answer certain questions. Can absentee ballots be used? Does the church distinguish between voting members and nonvoting members (such as youth under eighteen)? Can constituents of long standing vote? What percentage of the vote is needed for the call? Should the vote be unanimous? Will there be a paper ballot? Can the congregation vote twice if the first ballot is close?

17

If the candidate is accepted, the committee has accomplished a great task, and it is finished. A telephone call should be made, and a formal call letter should be sent (Item M, p. 89). A letter should be sent to any candidate still being held as a possible candidate. If the church does not accept the candidate, return to Steps Seven and Eight. If you have no other candidates, return to Step One.

STEP ELEVEN—The completion of responsibilities

Upon a church's voting favorably and a candidate's accepting the call, two items of business are necessary:

1. Notify the state and national association (GARBC) concerning the calling of the pastor, present address, date of arrival, first Sunday in the pulpit, and the date of the installation service.
2. Make appropriate plans for the installation service (Item O, p. 93).

Conclusion

May the Lord give both your pastor and the people many years of exciting ministry together in your church and community. Please check over the letter list (Item P, p. 95) to assure that you have not failed to notify any potential candidate who may believe he is still being considered.

CHAPTER 3

Considerations for Calling Additional Staff

The calling of an associate staff member is a process that must bring into focus many different issues, needs, and variables. The goal is to develop a team of staff members who will complement one another in the areas of skills and gifts and who will also be harmonious in the process of ministering. Staff members who do not function as intended will have unmet expectations from the congregation. This lack leads to frustration and friction.

When a Congregation Should Consider Calling Additional Staff

Churches should consider a second staff position when the attendance runs between 150 and 225. One of the problems in breaking the 150 to 225 attendance barrier has to do with the amount of support programming carried on by the church. The tendency is for only a few people to be involved in the leadership of all of the activities. These people become tired and lose their creativity. Consequently they are unable to facilitate a program adequate to meet the needs of 150-plus people. A church with one pastoral staff is unable to expand its program because the pastor is involved in too many activities to do anything well.

The associate position becomes a necessity if a church is going to reach its community adequately for Christ. In congregations of several thousand, the ratio of pastoral staff to member/attenders may be a little smaller than one staff for every 150 to 200 attenders. Great consideration should be given to the needs of the attenders, as well as to the needs of the members.

Obviously larger congregations will have more specialized programs than smaller congregations with a narrower focus. For example, in a very large church a youth pastor might be responsible for only one age group.

What a Congregation Should Consider in Calling Additional Staff

When looking for a second staff person, churches often make false assumptions about their needs. How does a church determine need? Obviously many individuals and groups have a vested interest in the process. Several studies will help determine the needs.

1. Study how to facilitate and *support the senior pastor* in building up the areas where he does not have his greatest strengths.

   A mistake that a church can make is to misinterpret areas of growth in the church.

People will see a specific program of their church growing rapidly. Usually this is because of the gifts and abilities of the senior pastor. Intending to help the pastor, the congregation will find someone to minister in the area in which he is strong. They have not misread the growth factor; they have misread the need factor. They should accommodate areas of the church where weaknesses persist.

Another problem may arise when you call a man to minister where the pastor has his greatest strength. Hiring such a man sets in motion processes that steal needed strokes from the pastor. This situation often causes paranoia on the part of one or both staff members. Both try to work in the same areas, and each feels threatened by the other.

It would be well if the pastor would list his strengths and "non-strengths" from a subjective point of view. The board, or those appointed by the board, should do a separate evaluation of the pastor's strengths and "non-strengths." When both the pastor and the board/committee have finished their evaluations, the pastor and two members from the board should review the study to determine what areas can be enhanced so that the ministry can be strengthened.

2. Study the church body.

A committee should work on demographics *within the church* to find the weaknesses and to learn where the church is not meeting the expectations of the people (Items B, D1, and D2, pp. 27, 33, 39). A careful evaluation of the weaknesses, expectations, and needs must be made to develop a profile for a new position. A review of the fellowship groups in your church and to whom they minister is valuable. This review will help you determine who is being left out of the church's ministry.

3. Consider carefully the demographics of the community.

A church needs to look at its community. Who is out there? What are their needs? How can the church best meet those needs? Sometimes churches avoid looking at their community because of the problems they find, that is, problems associated with divorce, singleness, single-parent families, and so on. Again, may I emphasize that you need the same information and statistics about the community as you do about members and attenders. You need to know if your church reflects the community. If your church is totally different, evaluate why it is different. Perhaps your church is behind a decade or so in its relationship to the community.

The church should consider a number of areas concerning the community and its needs. The neighborhood might be a developing community with a considerable number of children under the age of junior high. It may be a community of double-income couples without children. It could be a community with an older population. In fact, many senior citizens today are lonely because no one touches their lives.

After the church has evaluated the gifts and abilities of the senior pastor, the unmet needs within the local church, and the demographics of the community, it can begin planning the profile for the ministry of the new staff person.

How a Congregation Should Proceed in Calling Additional Staff

It would be wise for the church to set up several subcommittees to work independently in the three previously mentioned areas: needs of the pastor, needs of the congregation, and needs of the community. Three studies conducted independently will develop a more objective evaluation than if one group does all three. It is easy for a committee to build patterns and set up convenient comparisons that are not necessarily true.

You have a threefold desire in this research:

1. You want to have a greater impact in the community for Jesus Christ.
2. You want to meet the needs of believers within the church so that they can grow and become more mature Christians. This growth involves a great variety of activities from fellowship groups and small Bible studies to care units and task/ministry activities. All these activities and groups should be administered and directed by a full-time vocational person within the church.
3. You also need to consider the senior pastor and do that which will enhance and strengthen his ministry. Perhaps the senior pastor is strong in preaching and in ministering to young people. At this particular point it may be a mistake to look for a youth man. On the other hand, after consultation with the pastor, you might decide that it would be appropriate. He would then be able to focus his skills more toward the general shepherding of the flock.

As to developing the material and processing the formation, follow the steps for calling a pastor in this manual (chap. 2, pp. 12–18).

The Job Description a Church Should Design in Calling Additional Staff

A great variety of ministries exist within today's church. In addition, a great variety of positions have evolved through the years. These variations bring a multitude of different job descriptions to church ministries. I believe the job description must reflect the church's character and vision. One mistake that churches make is to devise a job description so rigid that individuals feel they are fenced in and unable to function well within the body. Another mistake is to have no job description at all. Anything and everything the senior pastor and everybody else doesn't want to do becomes part of the responsibility of the associate or the assistant.

Expectations need to be clearly written for each staff member. The reason I prefer to use the term "expectations" rather than "job description" is that job descriptions carry an employer/employee mentality. Job descriptions do not give the individual much ownership in what he/she is doing. The associates or assistants need to have ownership in their ministry so that they deal more in the area of feeling. We know that certain objective tasks and goals must be accomplished and that they need to be listed carefully. But there are also subjective things that need to happen in the lives of the people with whom you work; however, they often do not come through in a job description.

Positions Churches Usually Consider in Calling Additional Staff

The following is a short list of types of ministry titles found in churches. Often two or more are in the title and job description of one staff person.

1. Children's Worker

This category usually includes young people in sixth or seventh grade and under.

The programming can include Sunday School, club work, summer camp, summer Bible classes (Vacation Bible School), and so on.

2. Youth Pastor

A youth pastor position can be divided into several categories. Some churches have a youth pastor for junior high and another one for senior high. Other churches have a youth pastor for both junior and senior high youth. Still other churches combine all the youth from junior high through college and young career people.

One fact that a youth pastor must be aware of is that his call includes more than being a social director. He is called to be a youth pastor. Obviously young people need many social activities. At this time in their lives they are looking for fellowship and enjoyment. If a church fails to meet these needs, the young people will turn to unhelpful secular activities, or they will find their way to another church. In addition to the social emphasis, however, young people need in-depth Bible study and discipleship training. The most fruitful opportunity for a youth pastor is to develop disciples of his young people. Those who are discipled carefully will become solid Christian workers in the years to come. Balance is a key factor.

A youth pastor will be an "out of the office people person." These expectations need to be understood so that when people call the church, they don't expect him always to be in his office. For the church to expect a youth pastor to be in the office eight hours during the day is unrealistic. He will spend much time with his young people and many evenings away from his family. This schedule will probably be more true of the youth pastor than of the other staff people in the church.

3. Singles Ministry

Today a great need exists for a singles ministry in the church. The demographics of our society show that the number of singles is constantly growing, either by the procrastination of young people to get married until later in life or by the tendency of married couples to get a divorce. Singles have a great variety of unusual needs. First, they need sound advice and direction. Second, they are often lonely people looking for relational input in their lives. Third, they are one of the most creative and energetic groups of people with which one can work.

A singles ministry is not a "uni-interest" ministry. College-age singles are becoming more serious in their consideration for a mate and life work. Committed singles are now moving on into the late 20s and early 30s. They don't mix very well with those who are in the late teens and early 20s. Some singles, because of divorce or other circumstances, are single parents. They have a whole new arena of needs far different from the young singles or the older singles. Single parents are often more vulnerable because they have a lot of extra stress. Thus you need to know what kind of singles' group you are planning to reach. You should understand that you can't put them all in one "bunch."

4. Counseling

Over the past twenty-five years, counseling has become one of the major ministries for a pastor. Counseling often consumes many hours of the pastor's time. He may desperately need to be assisted in this duty so that he can redirect his efforts to other areas.

5. Administration

In years past the church was a quiet, local, closely related body functioning within a small and stable community. It has become a body drawn together by a common bond in Jesus Christ yet living in a mobile, changing society with predominantly surface relationships. Although the average size of church membership in the United States may be less than 100 members, many churches have moved from 75 constituents to 250 or even to several thousand. This range has made it necessary to develop a specialized ministry of administration.

It is interesting to note the structure of older church buildings. They didn't have church offices. Many times they didn't even have a study. The pastor was the man in their homes shepherding his people. Today we have church offices, with an office for each staff member. Offices are not viewed as studies; the pastor finds it difficult, almost impossible to study. He needs his own personal library, where he can find quiet time to study. Administration probably consumes from 40 to more than 60 percent of a pastor's time, which is a lot of time given over to details. This time factor obviously relates directly to the size of the church body. Thus, as a church grows larger, administrative leadership is important.

The congregation should evaluate its membership to determine if lay leadership could assume various areas of administration. Some church boards are adequate and merely need to be given the opportunity to minister in this way.

6. Minister of Music

Music is and has been an important factor within a church, especially for worship. People's needs are often met by good music that prepares them for the spoken Word. Their hearts are touched, and they focus more quickly on worship as they come together with good music. It seems that churches with an effective musical program benefit greatly, and people are blessed. Certainly the ministry of music is an important factor in the church. If you do not have people in your body to facilitate or draw together a good music program, a music minister may be an important addition to your staff.

7. Christian Education Director

A Christian education director is one who orchestrates, plans, and administers the educational program of the church. This person should have a clear understanding of the church's philosophy and may even need to develop an educational philosophy for the church. The Christian education director must have a positive understanding of his/her own philosophy and leadership style so he/she can give precise direction to your body. You will find that a C.E. director is probably more of a "desk and paper-centered person." This fact must be understood. Clearly express these expectations to the church body before you call a person to this position.

Beginning the Process of Calling an Additional Staff Member

As to developing the material and processing the information, follow the instructions and steps for calling a pastor (chap. 2, pp. 12–18).

Community demographic material is often available for a small fee from your local Chamber of Commerce. You may also find the information in your local library.

Timeline

Because 75 percent of all placement is accomplished within a year, this timeline has been set up on a fifty-two-week schedule. It should be noted that 50 percent of all rural and small town churches complete the placement process within six months. Fifty-five percent of all urban churches take more than a year. You may wish to modify this schedule accordingly.

It is good to monitor your progress so that you will not procrastinate. If you are ahead of schedule, readjust all remaining time. It would be well to color in the appropriate weekly schedule as you finish each phase and each step. This visual representation will give you an idea of how well you are proceeding.

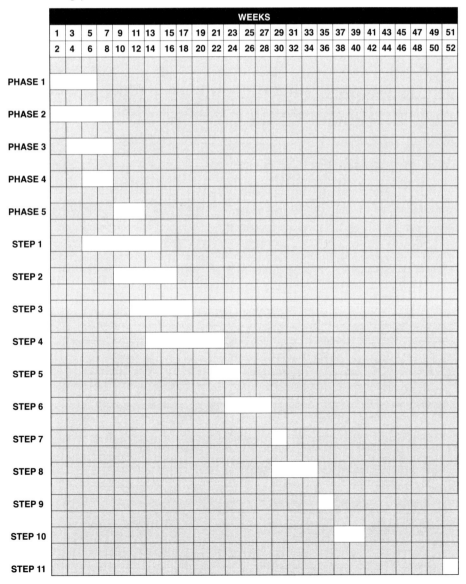

Church and Community Information

The pastoral search committee must have a clear understanding of all aspects of the church and community. They should do research to be fully informed. The committee should divide this assignment among the members to facilitate the task. The committee may obtain outside help by asking people not on the committee to help gather the material.

Church History

1. Origin and date
2. Factors of growth and development
3. Any major changes in affiliation or doctrine
4. Former pastors—length of ministry, strength of church at time (Item C, p. 31)
5. Major occupations of constituency
6. Lay leadership evaluation
7. Any major issues of change during last ten years

Church Statistics

8. Present membership

   ____ Sunday School   ____ Morning worship service

   ____ Evening service   ____ Prayer meeting

   ____ Youth fellowship   ____ Women's fellowship

   ____ Men's fellowship   ____ other _____

9. Attendance for past year

   ____ Sunday School   ____ Morning worship service

   ____ Evening service   ____ Prayer meeting

   ____ Youth fellowship   ____ Women's fellowship

   ____ Men's fellowship   ____ other _____

10. Income and budget for past five years

Year	Income	Budget

11. Growth pattern for past five years

Below, record the average Sunday School attendance for the year, the average morning worship service attendance for the year, and the church membership. Add the three and then divide by three.

Year	Attendance	Year	Attendance

(S.S. + A.M. Worship + Membership ÷ 3 = _____)

12. Growth pattern for next ten years
   a. Projected growth pattern for next five years _____
   b. Projected growth pattern for next ten years _____

13. Church membership/attender demographic information
   a. Age and gender

Age	Male	Female
0–5		
6–11		
12–19		
19–21		
22–29		
30–39		
40–49		
50–55		
56–64		
65+		

   b. Number of two-parent homes _____
   c. Number of single-parent homes _____
   d. Median income per household _____

14. Groups ministering to each area in #13

   _____   _____
   _____   _____
   _____   _____

15. Occupation evaluation

_____ Management   _____ Professional

_____ Office or sales   _____ Medical

_____ Industrial worker   _____ Education

_____ Construction worker   _____ Unemployed

_____ Agriculture   _____ Other _____

Church Property

16. Size of property _____

17. Seating of auditorium _____

18. Christian education facilities _____

19. Description of parsonage (if applicable)

_____ Number of rooms   _____ Number of bedrooms

_____ Appliances   _____ Features

_____ Other _____

20. Age and condition of building _____

21. Indebtedness _____

Church Community

Your church should take into consideration more than just the members and attenders from your stated city/community boundaries. To have a true picture of the extent of your church's community, locate the farthest regular-attending member. With the church at center, use the distance to the member as a general guide for the radius of a circle. The area within the circle is your church's community.

22. Population statistics

    a. Total number of people living within your church's community _____

    b. Age and gender

Age	Male	Female
0–5		
6–11		
12–19		
19–21		
22–29		
30–39		
40–49		
50–55		
56–64		
65+		

c. Number of two-parent homes _____

d. Number of single-parent homes _____

e. Median income per household _____

23. Growth pattern
    a. Projected growth pattern for next five years _____
    b. Projected growth pattern for next ten years _____

24. Type or combination of types of community
    _____ rural   _____ urban   _____ suburban

25. Major industries _____

    _____

26. Occupation evaluation
    _____ Management   _____ Professional
    _____ Office or sales   _____ Medical
    _____ Industrial worker   _____ Education
    _____ Construction worker   _____ Unemployed
    _____ Agriculture   Other _____

27. Other churches within your community

    _____
    _____
    _____

ITEM C

Pastoral History of the Church

It would be well to assign a different pastor in your church's history to each committee member for research. You will find this exercise will tell you more about the church than it will about your pastors. If the cycle of ministry reveals a short tenure for every pastor, there is a problem within the church that needs to be discovered. If the same or similar reason for a former pastor's leaving is registered for each pastor, some situations must be understood about the church.

Name of Pastor	Dates of Ministry	Length of Ministry	Strength of Pastor (i.e., preaching, loved people, evangelist, etc.)	Major Strength of Church during Ministry	Major Weakness of Church during Ministry	Reason Pastor Left (e.g., asked to resign, felt time to leave, pressure to to leave, asked to larger opportunity, etc.)

Congregational Survey

(Be sure to include a comment sheet with this questionnaire.)

Personal Profile

(Please check the information that applies to you.)

1. Church membership. Are you a
   _____ member?   _____ nonmember?

2. Age. How old are you?
   _____ 16–17
   _____ 18–25
   _____ 26–35
   _____ 36–50
   _____ 51–65
   _____ 65+

3. Gender. Are you
   _____ male?   _____ female?

4. Marital status. Are you
   _____ single (never married)?   _____ married?   _____ widowed?
   _____ separated?   _____ divorced?

5. Children. If you have children,
   how many live with you? _____
   What is the number in each age group?
   _____ 1–5   _____ 6–12   _____ 13–18   _____ 18+

6. Occupation. Into which category does your occupation fit?
   _____ managerial   _____ professional   _____ skilled labor
   _____ general labor   _____ student   _____ retired
   _____ homemaker   _____ unemployed   _____ other (please specify)_____

7. Church attendance.

    Which services do you attend?

    _____ Sunday School   _____ Sunday morning service

    _____ Sunday evening service   _____ weeknight prayer

    _____ Bible study

    What is the total number of years you have attended this church?

    _____ 0–5   _____ 6–10   _____ 10+

8. Church activities. Are you serving in at least one church-related activity (i.e., choir; teaching Sunday School, club, etc.) ?

    _____ yes   _____ no

9. Education. What is the highest level you have completed?

    _____ high school   _____ college   _____ postgraduate

10. Travel.

    What is your out-of-town travel time during one year (work and vacation)?

    _____ 0–10%   _____ 11–30%   _____ 30%+

    How many Sundays per year are you away?

    _____ 0–5   _____ 6–10   _____ 10+

11. Future church attendance. How many years in the future do you think you will be attending this church?

    _____ 1–3   _____ 4–6   _____ 6+

Spiritual Needs

*(Place a check beside the needs that pertain to you but are **not presently being satisfied**.)*

_____ assurance of forgiveness

_____ assurance of salvation

_____ basic Christian doctrine

_____ Bible knowledge

_____ development of personal ministry skills (e.g., witnessing, discipling, group leadership)

_____ family devotions

_____ family relationships

_____ help in leading an obedient/victorious lifestyle

_____ knowledge of God—His attributes

_____ prayer—how to

_____ quiet time—establishing with consistency

_____ Scripture memorization

_____ stewardship of time and money—understanding and practicing

_____ other (please use comment sheet)

Personal Needs

*(Place a check beside the needs that pertain to you but are **not presently being satisfied**.)*

_____ Christian fellowship/social—seniors
_____ Christian fellowship/social—single parents
_____ Christian fellowship/social—others
_____ ministry to children of single parent families
_____ physical impairment, hearing/blind
_____ transportation for church and church activities
_____ transportation for personal needs
_____ other (please use comment sheet)

Pastoral Profile

Biographical Data

(Please check your preference in considering a potential pastoral candidate.)

1. Age. What age do you prefer the pastor to be?
   _____ -30   _____ 30–45   _____ 45–55
   _____ 55+   _____ does not matter

2. Marital status. What do you prefer for the pastor's family status?
   _____ single   _____ married, no children
   _____ married, with children   _____ does not matter

3. Education. What degree of education do you prefer for a pastor?
   _____ Bible school   _____ Bible college   _____ liberal arts college
   _____ seminary   _____ does not matter
   If you indicated seminary, please check your preference.
   _____ Baptist (please specify by name) _____
   _____ Other (please specify by name) _____

4. Wife's education. What level do you prefer your pastor's wife to have reached?
   _____ high school   _____ college   _____ postgraduate   _____ does not matter

5. Wife's involvement. What kind of involvement do you prefer the pastor's wife to have?
   _____ active in life of church
   _____ may have outside employment or career pursuit
   _____ not employed
   _____ does not matter

Professional Experience
(Check the answers with which you agree.)

6. Should the pastor have some experience in secular work?
_____ yes   _____ no   _____ does not matter

7. Should the pastor have experience in church work or on a pastoral staff?
_____ 0–4 years   _____ 4–10 years   _____ 10+ years   _____ does not matter

8. In which of the following areas of church work should the pastor have experience?
_____ preaching
_____ teaching
_____ counseling
_____ youth work
_____ visitation
_____ Christian education
_____ other (specify) _____

Personal Abilities
(In #9, please rank the abilities according to priority 1, 2, 3, etc. If you do not feel that specific interest need, do not mark it. Please answer #10.)

9. I believe that the most important ministry areas for which a pastor in our church needs abilities are these areas:
_____ handicap-impaired
_____ family
_____ day school
_____ singles
_____ seniors
_____ single parents
_____ Christian education
_____ youth work
_____ women's fellowship
_____ men's fellowship
_____ church fellowship—developing personal relationships
_____ community and social concerns
_____ missions—home and overseas
_____ other (specify) _____
_____ other (specify) _____

10. Above all other, what characteristic would you desire in your pastor?

_____

Doctrine and Affiliation

(Check the answers with which you agree.)

11. Should he believe and accept the doctrinal statement of our church's affiliation (GARBC)?

_____ yes _____ no

12. Should he agree and abide by our church's covenant and constitution?

_____ yes _____ no

13. Should he be involved in or supportive of state and national associations (as in the GARBC) and/or be willing to do so?

_____ yes _____ no

Church Objectives and Goals

To be effective in its ministry, a church must have a clear idea of its objectives and goals. The following questions are designed to stimulate your thinking and help define your vision of the role of our church in doing the work of our Lord Jesus Christ.

(Please be brief, and return this completed sheet to the pastoral search committee as soon as possible.)

14. What is the church?

_____
_____
_____

15. For what purpose does our church exist?

_____
_____
_____

16. How can we best achieve that purpose?

_____
_____
_____

17. What kind of pastor will best help us achieve that purpose?

_____
_____
_____

(If you have further information for the pastoral search committee, please write your comments on a separate sheet and return it in an envelope to the church office.)

Congregational Survey

The purpose of this survey is to provide our pastoral search committee with a better understanding as to the needs of individuals in our church. In the future, you will be given the opportunity to make formal suggestions concerning pastoral candidates.

Please check the information that applies to you. Place the appropriate letter in the space provided, then return the survey to _____ by _____.

Thanks for your prompt cooperation on completing this survey.

Personal Information

(Please place the appropriate letter in the space provided.)

_____ 1. Age: (A) -21 (B) 22–30 (C) 31–40 (D) 41–50 (E) 51–60 (F) 61–70 (G) 70+

_____ 2. Gender: (A) male (B) female

_____ 3. Marital status: (A) single (never married) (B) married (C) widowed (D) separated (E) divorced

4.–7. Family situation:

   (In the blank write the number of children living at home in each age group.)

   _____ 4. -5 years

   _____ 5. 6–12 years

   _____ 6. 13–18 years

   _____ 7. 18+ years

_____ 8. Wife's work: (A) part-time (B) full-time (C) does not work outside the home (D) not applicable

Personal Spiritual Involvement

_____ 9. Years I have been a Christian: (A) 0–1 (B) 2–4 (C) 5–9 (D) 10+

_____ 10. With regard to this church, I am (A) a member (B) a regular attender (C) looking it over.

_____ 11. If a member, for how many years? (A) 0–1 (B) 2–4 (C) 5–10 (D) 10+

_____ 12. Hours currently spent per week in Christian service related to our church: (A) 0 (B) 1–2 (C) 3–4 (D) 5–6 (E) 6+

_____ 13. I attend Sunday School at least (A) 4 (B) 3 (C) 2 (D) 1 Sunday(s) per month.

_____ 14. I attend morning worship at least (A) 4 (B) 3 (C) 2 (D) 1 Sunday(s) per month.

_____ 15. I attend evening service at least (A) 4 (B) 3 (C) 2 (D) 1 Sunday(s) per month.

_____ 16. I do personal Bible reading (A) 7 (B) 6–5 (C) 4–3 (D) 2–1 (E) 0 days per week.

_____ 17. I participate in personal prayer (A) 7 (B) 6–5 (C) 4–3 (D) 2–1 (E) 0 days per week.

_____ 18. Over the past year, I believe my spiritual health has (A) improved (B) stayed the same (C) deteriorated.

19.–23. The church in general:

(Answer the following questions with A—yes, B—to some extent, or C—no.)

_____ 19. Our church's activities help strengthen families.

_____ 20. I am aware of opportunities to use my spiritual gifts in this church.

_____ 21. The missions emphasis at our church has stimulated my interest.

_____ 22. I feel comfortable inviting friends to this church.

_____ 23. I have a strong desire to minister to others in my church/community.

24.–30. You and our church, your family, and others:

(Answer the following questions with A—often, B—to some extent, or C—rarely.)

_____ 24. I leave a worship service with a feeling that I worshiped God.

_____ 25. I am pleased with the style and quality of the music in my church.

_____ 26. I find that the preaching at this church speaks to my needs.

_____ 27. I participate in family devotions.

_____ 28. I spend time with non-Christian friends.

_____ 29. Over the past year, I have spoken to non-Christians about faith in Christ.

_____ 30. Relationships in my immediate family are characterized by warmth and respect.

Spiritual Needs

(Place a check beside the needs pertaining to you at present.)

_____ 31. Assurance of salvation

_____ 32. Basic Christian doctrine

_____ 33. Bible knowledge

_____ 34. Development of personal ministry

_____ 35. Family relationships

_____ 36. Help in leading an obedient, victorious lifestyle

_____ 37. Small group study

_____ 38. Stewardship of time and money

_____ 39. My importance in the Body of Christ

_____ 40. Reconciliation in the church fellowship

_____ 41. Understanding and using spiritual gifts and skills

_____ 42. Spiritual and physical healing

_____ 43. Biblical posture on justice in society

_____ 44. Other _____

Pastoral Profile

45., 46. Education and experience:

(Please share your preference in considering potential candidates for our pastor by placing the letter of your answer in the blank.)

_____ 45. Education. Should he have an advanced degree beyond seminary? (A) yes (B) no (C) does not matter

_____ 46. Years in ministry. How many years should he have pastored? (A) -10 years (B) 10–15 years (C) 15–20 years (D) 20+ years (E) does not matter

47.–58. Priorities:

*(These are personal priorities you believe are the most important priorities needed for a senior pastor in our church. Please identify your top **three** preferences—1, 2, 3.)*

_____ 47. Pulpit ministry

_____ 48. Evangelism/outreach

_____ 49. Discipleship

_____ 50. Teaching

_____ 51. Visionary leadership

_____ 52. Worldwide missions

_____ 53. Administration

_____ 54. Personal availability

_____ 55. Denominational leadership

_____ 56. Community and social needs

_____ 57. Other _____

_____ 58. Other _____

Observations

59., 60. Present:

59. The things I like best about our church are

_____

_____

_____

_____

60. The things I feel need the most improvement in our church are

_____

_____

_____

_____

61.–63. Future:

(Check one of the following completions to this statement: In the future, I would like to see the numerical size of our church . . .)

_____ 61. Remain about the same

_____ 62. Increase

63. Other comments

(If you have further input for the pastoral search committee, please write your comments on a separate sheet and return it in an envelope to the church office.)

Flow Chart of Calling Procedure

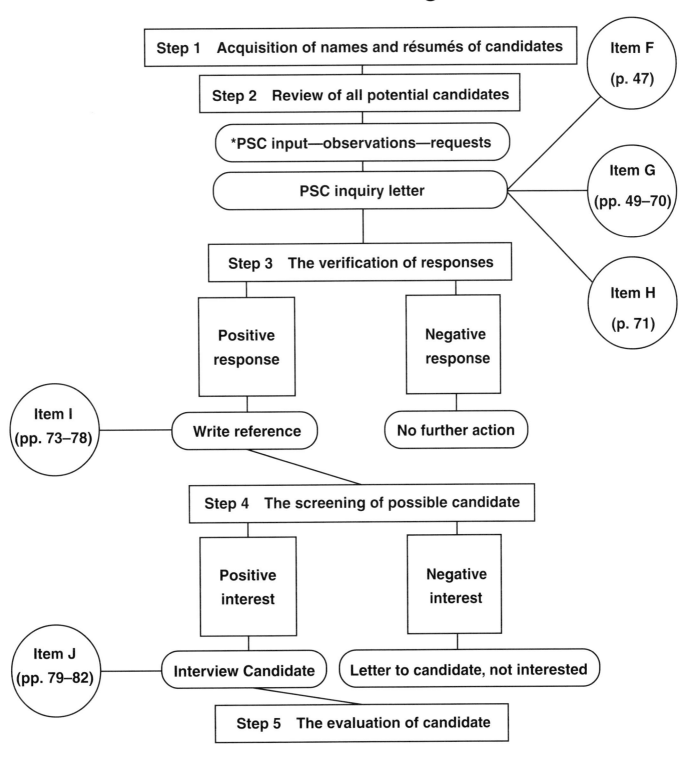

Step 1   Acquisition of names and résumés of candidates

Item F (p. 47)

Step 2   Review of all potential candidates

*PSC input—observations—requests

PSC inquiry letter

Item G (pp. 49–70)

Item H (p. 71)

Step 3   The verification of responses

Positive response

Negative response

Item I (pp. 73–78)

Write reference

No further action

Step 4   The screening of possible candidate

Positive interest

Negative interest

Item J (pp. 79–82)

Interview Candidate

Letter to candidate, not interested

Step 5   The evaluation of candidate

*PSC—Pastoral Search Committee

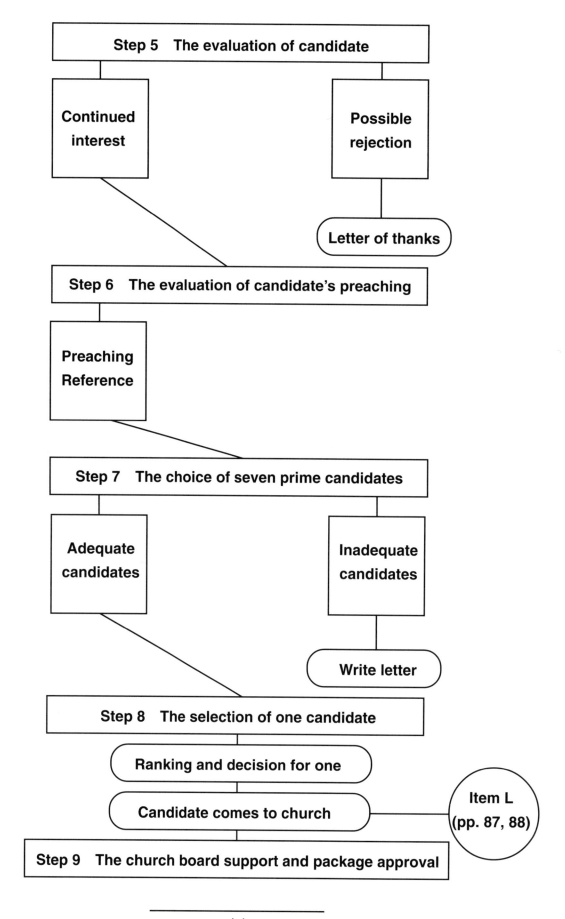

Step 5   The evaluation of candidate

Continued interest

Possible rejection

Letter of thanks

Step 6   The evaluation of candidate's preaching

Preaching Reference

Step 7   The choice of seven prime candidates

Adequate candidates

Inadequate candidates

Write letter

Step 8   The selection of one candidate

Ranking and decision for one

Candidate comes to church

Item L (pp. 87, 88)

Step 9   The church board support and package approval

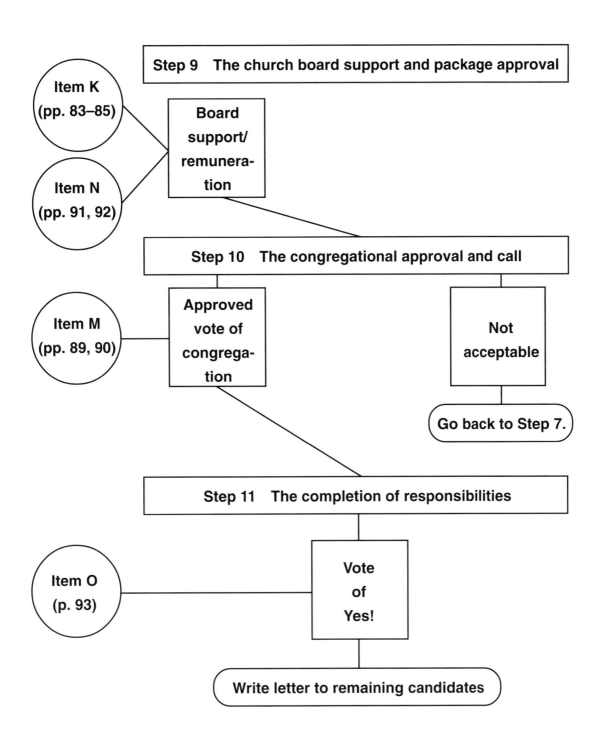

Step 9   The church board support and package approval

Item K
(pp. 83–85)

Item N
(pp. 91, 92)

Board
support/
remunera-
tion

Step 10   The congregational approval and call

Item M
(pp. 89, 90)

Approved
vote of
congrega-
tion

Not
acceptable

Go back to Step 7.

Step 11   The completion of responsibilities

Item O
(p. 93)

Vote
of
Yes!

Write letter to remaining candidates

Sample Letter
to Possible Pastoral Candidates

(Include this letter with the questionnaire.)

Rev. _____

0000 Any Street

Somewhere, U.S.A.

Dear Pastor _____:

Our pastor, _____, has accepted a call to another position, leaving us without a minister. A pulpit committee has been formed to seek and recommend a successor.

Your name has been recommended to us as someone who could give us the needed leadership in our church. We are, therefore, interested in obtaining more information from you.

Without any commitment on your part or on the part of this church, we would like to know whether you are willing to be considered as a possible candidate.

If you answer in the affirmative, we ask you to complete the enclosed questionnaire and return it to us within ten days. If you do not feel led to consider this opportunity, please return the questionnaire to us.

Enclosed are some items that will give you insight into our church, our ministries, and our community.

Should you have any questions, please call me collect at _____, and I will be happy to give you further information.

Sincerely in Christ,

_____

Pastoral Search Committee Chairman

Enclosures: Questionnaire, information sheets on church and community

---

(NOTE TO PULPIT COMMITTEE: It is a good gesture to enclose a self-addressed, stamped envelope with this letter.)

ITEM G₁

Minister's Profile Information—
Subjective

This form should be sent to serious candidates. You may either make out a form or have the potential candidate write a paper following the format of these guidelines.

Subjective Profile

1. Name: _____

2. Address: _____

3. Date of birth: _____

  (month) (day) (year)

4. Wife's name: _____

5. Date of marriage: _____

6. Children:

Name(s)	Date(s) of Birth

7. Wife's training and major interest:

8. Share how you make family a priority:

9. Describe your health:

10. Education:

School	Degree	Year Obtained

11. Give a brief summary of your conversion experience:

12. Give a brief summary of your call to the ministry:

13. We desire a copy of the theological paper you prepared for your license/ordination. If this paper is unavailable, please share your theological position in relation to our Statement of Faith. (Use separate paper and attach it to this sheet.)

14. Your current church:

Name _____

Membership _____

Average church attendance _____

Sunday School attendance _____

Church budget _____

Annual giving to missions _____

Listing of staff positions

What ministries do you have to children and youth?

What other services do you have in your church in addition to the Sunday morning worship service?

Do you conduct a midweek service, or do you have small groups?

15. Prior churches served:

Church/ Organization	Location	Dates	Position

16. How do you view your involvement with various segments of the church? (Use separate paper and attach it to this sheet.)

17. Describe your expectations and philosophy of team relationships within a multiple staff. Describe your understanding of congregational church government and whether you can ascribe to it. (Use separate paper and attach it to this sheet.)

18. In what order would you rank your strengths in ministry? (Use 1 to indicate your greatest strength. Please rank all items.)

____ Christian education   ____ Fund-raising

____ Church administration   ____ Leading in worship

____ Church growth   ____ Missions promotion

____ Community service   ____ Pastoral care and calling

____ Denominational/Associational (GARBC   ____ Personal counseling

    and state association) service   ____ Preaching

____ Discipling laymen   ____ Social action

____ Equipping believers   ____ Youth ministry

____ Evangelism   ____ Other _____

19. What do you believe is your greatest personal strength?

20. What do you see as your ministerial weaknesses, which will need support from laymen or other staff?

21. What ministerial credentials do you presently hold?
    License Date: _____ Denomination/Affiliation:_____
    Ordination Date: _____ Denomination/Affiliation:_____

22. List Association (GARBC) committees, boards, and positions in which you have been involved.

23. Please give the names and addresses of personal references whom we could contact.

Person	Name	Address	Phone Number
A colleague in the Fellowship			
A leader in your present church			
Someone who has worked under you			

24. Please enclose a recent picture of yourself and, if possible, of your wife and family.

Thank you for returning this questionnaire. Be assured that the information will be handled with discretion by the pulpit search committee.

**ON A SEPARATE SHEET OF PAPER,
PLEASE ANSWER THE FOLLOWING QUESTIONS:**

1. Have you ever been asked to resign from your church? If so, give details.
2. What other special Christian work experiences have you had?
3. What, if any, overseas or cross-cultural ministry experiences have you had?
4. What are your special interests and hobbies?
5. What is your chief contact with non-Christians?
6. List any community organizations (civic, social, etc.) of which you have been a member.
7. List any activities in which you participate that involve other churches.
8. List any Associational or pastors' meetings you attend and support.
9. What periodicals do you read regularly?
10. What books have had an impact upon your life during this past year?
11. List the books or articles you have written for publication.
12. Would you need special considerations because of involvement with other organizations or because of writing or speaking commitments?
13. What three persons have had the greatest positive impact on your life, and why?
14. What is your method of preaching? manuscript? notes? outline? without notes? topical? expository? textual? other (describe)?
15. Describe the place that worship should have in the church program.
16. In your pulpit ministry, how do you apply Scripture to life needs?
17. How do you see your ministry in equipping the saints? from the pulpit? in small groups? in personal discipling? other (describe)?
18. What are your spiritual gifts?
19. What do you think concerning the more controversial gifts of the Spirit (sign gifts)?
20. What is your view of women in positions of church leadership?
21. What role do contemporary theological and ethical issues play in your ministry?
22. What do you see as the important social issues the church faces today?
23. To what extent would these ethical and social issues occupy your preaching and teaching?
24. What is your view toward use of tobacco and alcoholic beverages?
25. How have you expanded your own view of the world or your missionary goals this past year?
26. What place does world evangelism have in your overall pulpit ministry?
27. How would you plan to deal with church growth and the formation of daughter churches?
28. How do you view your role as senior pastor as pertaining to the following areas?

Christian education	Music
Youth ministry	Financial stewardship
Evangelism	Pastoral and intern staff
Missions	Administration
Counseling	Church board
Visitation	

Minister's Profile Information—Objective

(Enclose a GARBC doctrinal statement to accompany #56 on page 66.)

Basic Church Interest Information

*(Please type or **clearly** print all information. **Circle your responses/answers to questions with multiple-choice answers.** Follow any additional instructions.)*

1. Title (Rev., Dr., Mr., Mrs., Ms.) Name _____

   (Last)   (First)   (Middle Initial)

2. Address _____

   (where you desire correspondence to be sent)

   _____

3. City, State, Zip _____

4. Home Phone_____

   May we call you there?   a. Yes   b. No

5. Office Phone _____

   May we call you there?   a. Yes   b. No

6. Gender: a. Male b. Female

7. What is your present interest in placement?

   a. I am presently **between** ministries and actively seeking placement.

   b. I am presently **in a ministry** and actively seeking placement.

   c. I am not actively seeking placement, but I am open to the possibility of moving if the right position were to become available.

   d. I am still in school but graduating soon and looking for placement.

   e. I am interested in internship or ministry while in school or working.

   f. I am not interested in another position at this time.

8. The position(s) I am (might be) interested in, in order of priority, are *(choose a church size for each position).*

Position	Church Size			
	a. 0–75	b. 75–200	c. 200–400	d. 400+
	a. 0–75	b. 75–200	c. 200–400	d. 400+
	a. 0–75	b. 75–200	c. 200–400	d. 400+

9. I'm looking for a ministry that is . . .   a. Full time   b. Part time

10. I'm **willing** to take a part-time position for a year or two.   a. Yes   b. No

11. Regarding the confidentiality of my interest in placement, . . .

    a. My desire for placement is already public. You may discuss this with anyone who is interested.

    b. My desire for placement is known only by a few. Please discuss this only with my board and with interested churches, asking that they keep it strictly confidential.

    c. No one knows of my interest. Please do not discuss this with anyone but me. Then I will decide whom to inform.

12. Regarding geographical location for ministry, . . .

    a. My choices for **region** of the country where I would like to work, in order of priority, are (rank them from 1—most desirable, to 6—least desirable).

    _____ Northwest

    _____ Southwest

    _____ North Central

    _____ South Central

    _____ Northeast

    _____ Southeast

    b. The three states where I'd prefer to minister, **in order of priority**, are

    1. _____

    2. _____

    3. _____

    c. These geographical preferences are . . . (Circle the entire answer.)

    very important to me

    not very important

    unimportant either way; I'd be willing to move to most places.

Basic Biographical Data

*(Please type or **clearly** print all information. Circle your responses/answers to questions with multiple-choice answers. Follow any additional instructions.)*

13. Date of Birth _____
    (Month)   (Day)   (Year)

14. Place of Birth _____
    (City)   (State or Province)   (Country)

15. Marital Status: a. Single   b. Married   c. Widowed
    d. Separated/Divorced   e. Remarried
    (If separated/divorced/remarried, please explain on a separate sheet.)

16. If married, give spouse's full (including maiden) name.

    _____
    (First)   (Maiden)   (Last)

17. Give your children's names and years of birth.

Name	Date

18. Your education (above high school).

School	Degree/Certificate	Date

19. Are there any special health needs in your family?   a. Yes   b. No
    (If yes, briefly describe below.)

Family Member	Health Need

20. Do you presently own your own home?   a. Yes   b. No

21. In your next position, do you prefer to
    a. Purchase your own home?
    b. Rent?
    c. Live in a parsonage?

22. Salary *(Complete the chart below.)*

	Present	Requested
Annual Salary		
Health Insurance Cost		
Life Insurance Cost		
Housing Allowance		
Personal Development		
Pension		
Other _____		
Other _____		
Other _____		

23. Car Allowance
    a. Present Car Allowance _____
    b. Requested Car Allowance _____

24. Other than your house, your car, and the debts you will pay off in the next two months, do you have outstanding debts in excess of $1,000?   a. Yes   b. No
    If yes, please explain. _____
    _____
    _____

25. Are you presently bivocational?   a. Yes   b. No
26. If yes, what is your other vocation?   _____
27. Are you willing to be bivocational?   a. Yes   b. No
28. Is your spouse planning and/or willing to work to improve your financial situation?
    a. Yes   b. No
29. Have you ever raised your personal financial support?   a. Yes   b. No
30. Are you willing to raise your personal financial support?   a. Yes   b. No
31. Are you bilingual?   a. Yes   b. No
    If yes, which languages? _____
    Is your spouse bilingual?   a. Yes   b. No
    If yes, which languages? _____
32. Would you **prefer** to minister to a culture other than the average white American culture?   a. Yes   b. No
33. Would you **be willing** to minister to a culture other than the average white American culture?   a. Yes   b. No
34. If you answered yes to questions 31 or 32, please list **in priority** the culture(s) you might minister to.
    a. _____
    b. _____
    c. _____

Ministry Experience

*(Please type or **clearly** print all information. **Circle your responses/answers to questions with multiple-choice answers.** Follow any additional instructions.)*

35. Are you   a. Licensed   b. Ordained   c. Neither?

36. If you are licensed or ordained, with whom? _____

37. Below please list your experience in the last five (or fewer if you have served in fewer) churches or ministries in which you ministered. **Start with the *most* recent.**

I.

a. Church Name _____

b. Church Address _____
         (City)   (State or Province)   (Zip Code or Postal Zone)

c. Phone Number _____

d. Date Hired _____
         (Month)   (Year)

e. Date Left _____
        (Month)   (Year)

f. Reason for Leaving _____

_____

_____

g. Your Position _____

h. Worship Attendance _____
         (When You Came)   (When You Left)

i. Percentage _____
         (White Collar)   (Blue Collar)

j. Location of Church *(Circle your answer.)*

     Inner-city

     Urban

     Suburban

     Rural

k. Your Experiences *(Describe them.)* _____

_____

_____

_____

_____

_____

_____

_____

_____

l. Your Accomplishments *(List them.)* _____

_____

_____

_____

_____

II.

a. Church Name _____

b. Church Address _____
                        (City)   (State or Province)   (Zip Code or Postal Zone)

c. Phone Number _____

d. Date Hired _____
             (Month)   (Year)

e. Date Left _____
           (Month)   (Year)

f. Reason for Leaving _____

   _____

   _____

g. Your Position _____

h. Worship Attendance _____
                 (When You Came)   (When You Left)

i. Percentage _____
            (White Collar)   (Blue Collar)

j. Location of Church *(Circle your answer.)*

   Inner-city

   Urban

   Suburban

   Rural

k. Your Experiences *(Describe them.)* _____

   _____

   _____

   _____

   _____

   _____

   _____

   _____

   _____

   _____

l. Your Accomplishments *(List them.)* _____

   _____

   _____

   _____

   _____

III.

a. Church Name _____

b. Church Address _____
                        (City)   (State or Province)   (Zip Code or Postal Zone)

c. Phone Number _____

d. Date Hired _____
             (Month)   (Year)

e. Date Left _____
           (Month)   (Year)

f. Reason for Leaving _____

_____

_____

g. Your Position _____

h. Worship Attendance _____
(When You Came)   (When You Left)

i. Percentage _____
(White Collar)   (Blue Collar)

j. Location of Church *(Circle your answer.)*

Inner-city

Urban

Suburban

Rural

k. Your Experiences *(Describe them.)* _____

_____

_____

_____

_____

_____

_____

_____

_____

_____

l. Your Accomplishments *(List them.)* _____

_____

_____

_____

_____

IV.

a. Church Name _____

b. Church Address _____
(City)   (State or Province)   (Zip Code or Postal Zone)

c. Phone Number _____

d. Date Hired _____
(Month)   (Year)

e. Date Left _____
(Month)   (Year)

f. Reason for Leaving _____

_____

_____

g. Your Position _____

h. Worship Attendance _____
(When You Came)   (When You Left)

i. Percentage _____
(White Collar)   (Blue Collar)

j. Location of Church *(Circle your answer.)*
    Inner-city
    Urban
    Suburban
    Rural
k. Your Experiences *(Describe them.)* _____

    _____

    _____

    _____

    _____

    _____

    _____

    _____

    _____

    _____

    _____

l. Your Accomplishments *(List them.)* _____

    _____

    _____

    _____

    _____

V.

a. Church Name _____

b. Church Address _____
            (City)   (State or Province)   (Zip Code or Postal Zone)

c. Phone Number _____

d. Date Hired _____
       (Month)   (Year)

e. Date Left _____
      (Month)   (Year)

f. Reason for Leaving _____

    _____

    _____

g. Your Position _____

h. Worship Attendance _____
         (When You Came)   (When You Left)

i. Percentage_____
      (White Collar)   (Blue Collar)

j. Location of Church *(Circle your answer.)*
    Inner-city
    Urban
    Suburban
    Rural

k. Your Experiences *(Describe them.)* _____

    _____

_____
_____
_____
_____
_____
_____
_____
_____
_____

l. Your Accomplishments *(List them.)* _____
_____
_____
_____
_____

38. Non-Pastoral Vocational Experience

Company	Your Title	Start Date	End Date	Area of Responsibility

39. Ministry Settings *(Use the following responses to describe your feelings about each ministry setting listed below.)*

Responses
1. I could be very fruitful here.
2. I could minister effectively here.
3. Ministry here would probably be difficult for me.
4. I would probably be unfruitful in this setting.

a. Inner City	1	2	3	4
b. Urban	1	2	3	4
c. Suburban	1	2	3	4
d. Independent City (under 50,000)	1	2	3	4
e. Small Town (under 20,000)	1	2	3	4
f. Rural (under 3,000)	1	2	3	4

40. Ministry Roles (*Use the following responses to rate your gifts/passions for each ministry role below.*)

> **Responses**
> 1. It is one of my greatest strengths.
> 2. I am strong here.
> 3. I am average here.
> 4. I am weak here.
> 5. It is one of my greatest weaknesses.

a. Shepherd/Pastor	1	2	3	4	5
b. Builder	1	2	3	4	5
c. Change Agent	1	2	3	4	5
d. Teacher	1	2	3	4	5
e. Counselor	1	2	3	4	5
f. Evangelist	1	2	3	4	5
g. Visionary Leader	1	2	3	4	5
h. Strategic Planner	1	2	3	4	5
i. Preacher	1	2	3	4	5
j. Church Planter	1	2	3	4	5

41. Ministry Emphasis (*Use the following responses to rate the emphasis [amount of time] you normally give to each of the following activities.*)

> **Responses**
> 1. Extremely important emphasis.
> 2. Important—I never slight this.
> 3. I do this when there is time.
> 4. I do this when I have to.
> 5. I avoid this if possible.

a. Preaching	1	2	3	4	5
b. Pastoral Care/Visitation	1	2	3	4	5
c. Administration/Planning	1	2	3	4	5
d. Missionary Promotion and Activities	1	2	3	4	5
e. Community Service	1	2	3	4	5

f.	Youth or Children's Ministry	1	2	3	4	5
g.	Social Action	1	2	3	4	5
h.	Public Worship	1	2	3	4	5
i.	Evangelism	1	2	3	4	5
j.	Christian Education	1	2	3	4	5
k.	Stewardship Development	1	2	3	4	5
l.	Training Leaders	1	2	3	4	5
m.	Small Group Discipleship	1	2	3	4	5
n.	One-on-One Discipleship	1	2	3	4	5
o.	Praying	1	2	3	4	5
p.	Managing/Supervising	1	2	3	4	5

Ethical and Social Issues

42. How would you characterize your marriage relationship?

a. Very strong   b. Strong   c. Average   d. Poor

43. How supportive of your ministry is your wife?

a. Very supportive—encourages me to persevere when I'm discouraged

b. Supportive—helps when I ask

c. Accepting—allows me to minister without hindering me

d. Reluctant—occasionally discourages me from continuing

e. Antagonistic—often encourages me to leave the ministry

44. To what extent is your spouse involved in your ministry?

a. Almost always leads some area of ministry

b. Occasionally leads a ministry

c. Almost always participates in some ministry

d. Sometimes participates in a ministry

e. Seldom participates in ministry but keeps the home fires burning

f. Never participates in ministry

45. Have you ever been involved in or convicted of child abuse?   a. Yes   b. No

46. Have you ever been involved in a homosexual lifestyle?   a. Yes   b. No

47. Have you ever been accused of sexual harassment?   a. Yes   b. No

Doctrinal and Ecclesiastical Issues

48. Have you read, do you agree with, and can you support the doctrinal statement of our state and national fellowships (GARBC)?   a. Yes   b. No

49. Do you support a congregational form of government?   a. Yes   b. No

50. Very briefly explain when, where, and how you were saved.

_____

_____

_____

_____

_____

51. Very briefly relate when, where, and how you were called to ministry.

_____

_____

_____

_____

_____

_____

52. Briefly explain how inerrancy of the Scriptures impacts your preaching.

_____

_____

_____

_____

_____

53. Briefly explain your position and practice (and that of your spouse, if it is different) concerning sign gifts, tongues, and healing.

_____

_____

_____

_____

_____

54. Briefly describe your position and practice (and that of your spouse, if it is different) on the role of women in the church.

_____

_____

_____

_____

_____

55. What is your attitude and practice (and that of your spouse, if it is different) concerning social drinking?

_____

_____

_____

_____

_____

_____

_____

56. Carefully read the GARBC's twenty-point doctrinal statement (enclosed) and then use the following responses to indicate your thinking regarding each statement.

Responses
1. Completely agree without reservation
2. Agree with some reservations
3. Disagree

a.	The Scriptures	1	2	3
b.	The True God	1	2	3
c.	The Holy Spirit	1	2	3
d.	The Devil, or Satan	1	2	3
e.	Creation	1	2	3
f.	The Fall of Man	1	2	3
g.	The Virgin Birth	1	2	3
h.	Salvation	1	2	3
i.	Resurrection and Priesthood of Christ	1	2	3
j.	Grace and the New Birth	1	2	3
k.	Justification	1	2	3
l.	Sanctification	1	2	3
m.	The Security of the Saints	1	2	3
n.	The Church	1	2	3
o.	Baptism and the Lord's Supper	1	2	3
p.	Separation	1	2	3
q.	Civil Government	1	2	3
r.	Israel	1	2	3
s.	Rapture and Subsequent Events	1	2	3
t.	The Righteous and the Wicked	1	2	3

57. Do you hold to all of the Baptist distinctives?
- B = Biblical Authority
- A = Autonomy of the Local Church
- P = Priesthood of All Believers
- T = Two Ordinances
- I = Individual Soul Liberty
- S = Saved, Baptized Church Membership
- T = Two offices
- S = Separation of Church and State

58. Are there **any** doctrinal positions you hold that **might** be regarded as outside the **mainstream** of fundamental Baptist teaching or practice?   a. Yes   b. No
(If yes, please explain.)

_____

_____

_____

_____

_____

_____

_____

_____

59. What percentage of the time do you practice each of the following preaching styles?
(Your answers should total 100%.)
_____ a. Expository, verse-by-verse
_____ b. Expository, passage-by-passage
_____ c. Expository, big idea
_____ d. Practical, important applications from this passage
_____ e. Topical, preach a topic from various passages
_____ f. Spiritual, preach whatever God lays on my heart
_____ g. Evangelistic, use each passage to lead into the gospel
_____ h. Other *(Describe.)* _____

_____

_____

60. Although none of the following may **fully** describe a church's responsibility, please place a 1, 2, and 3 by the three statements **you** think are the first, second, and third **most** important roles of a church.
_____ a. A platform to preach the Word
_____ b. A family to manifest love
_____ c. A community to promote justice
_____ d. A financial base for world missions
_____ e. An army to save the lost
_____ f. A temple in which to worship God
_____ g. A hospital to heal the afflicted
_____ h. A support base for individual "ministers"
_____ i. An equipping center to make disciples

61. **Briefly** describe the role of the senior pastor (as you see it) in a church of 500 to 1,000 attenders.

_____

_____

_____

_____

_____

_____

_____

_____

62. Briefly describe the leadership role of the pastor as a part of the church board.

_____

_____

_____

_____

_____

_____

_____

_____

63. Briefly describe the role and relationship of an associate pastor to the senior pastor.

_____

_____

_____

_____

_____

_____

_____

_____

_____

References

We will contact the following people as you have directed us in your answer to #11 regarding confidentiality.

PERSONAL REFERENCES—Two people (not related to you) whom you have known for more than ten years.

1. Name _____

    Day Phone _____ Night Phone _____

    Current Address _____

    | (City) | (State or Province) | (Zip or Postal Code) | (Country) |

2. Name _____

    Day Phone _____ Night Phone _____

    Current Address _____

    | (City) | (State or Province) | (Zip or Postal Code) | (Country) |

STAFF REFERENCES—two staff people who have worked **with** you in ministry.
(Please provide names from two churches if possible.)

1. Name _____

   Day Phone _____ Night Phone_____

   Current Address _____

   _____
   (City)   (State or Province)   (Zip or Postal Code)   (Country)

2. Name _____

   Day Phone _____ Night Phone_____

   Current Address _____

   _____
   (City)   (State or Province)   (Zip or Postal Code)   (Country)

CHURCH BOARD MEMBERS—two board members who have ministered with you in various churches.

1. Name _____

   Day Phone _____ Night Phone_____

   Current Address _____

   _____
   (City)   (State or Province)   (Zip or Postal Code)   (Country)

2. Name _____

   Day Phone _____ Night Phone_____

   Current Address _____

   _____
   (City)   (State or Province)   (Zip or Postal Code)   (Country)

Release Form

I agree that all information on this questionnaire and any accompanying questionnaires may be released to those seeking information regarding candidates for their church. I furthermore agree that interested persons may contact any references given, and I release any references form liability for information given.

_____   _____
Signature   Date

Suggested Materials to Send to the Prospective Candidate

The following information should be compiled and sent with other materials to the potential pastoral candidate to give him a look at your church and community. Each area should be assigned to a committee member or other church member for a research report.

Task	Person Assigned
1. Check to see if your Chamber of Commerce has material about your community. If so, send it.	
2. Compile statistics concerning your church, such as a. Average attendance for the last three years in all of the Sunday services, youth meetings, weekday children's activities, and any other regular or monthly meetings.	
b. Your church budget or giving for the last three years.	
c. Any plans for expansion.	
d. Details about any additional staff employed by your church, such as assistant pastor, secretary, custodian.	
3. A copy of your church constitution.	
4. A picture of the church, inside and out.	
5. If a parsonage is provided, draw an approximate floor plan on an $8\frac{1}{2}$" x 11" sheet; provide a picture of the exterior.	
6. Tell something concerning neighboring churches of your association and their distance from your church.	
7. Tell something concerning other community churches.	
8. Information about the school system, its size, location, etc.	
9. Describe the larger cities within a reasonable distance if your church happens to be rural or in a small town.	
10. General climatic conditions by seasons.	
11. A brief history of your church, such as its beginning, age, make up of membership, etc.	
12. Church demographics: The breakdown of church members and attenders by age, gender, marital status, education, occupation, church attendance, church involvement, spiritual needs.	

Task	Person Assigned
13. A church directory.	
14. Several copies of the monthly church letter, bulletins, and any other church literature.	
15. A schedule of regular programs/services/ministries of the church.	

Reference Questionnaire

(Enclose a self-addressed, stamped envelope with this questionnaire.)

This questionnaire is in reference to _____, who is being considered as a potential candidate of the _____ Church of _____, _____. Your honest response will be very valuable, and all information will be considered confidential.

Ministry

1. How long and in what connection have you known him?

   _____

   _____

   _____

2. To what extent does his wife support his ministry? *(Check the description that applies best.)*

   _____ She is very supportive.

   _____ She is supportive.

   _____ He is not married.

   _____ She would desire him in another vocation.

   _____ She is not excited about ministry.

3. In the following list, which **three areas** would you consider to be his strengths and/or "non-strengths"? *(Check Strength, "Non-strength," or Not Sure.)*

Item	Strength	"Non-strength"	Not Sure
Preaching			
Teaching			
Evangelism			
Visitation			
Discipleship			
Counseling			
Administration			
Personal relationships			
Leadership			

4. Do you regard him theologically . . . *(Check the appropriate description.)*
   ____ Moderately liberal
   ____ Middle of the road
   ____ Conservative
   ____ Fundamentalist

5. Is he evangelistic in his ministry? Explain your answer.

   _____

   _____

6. How do you consider him in the application of the gospel to the life and needs of the congregation? *(Check the appropriate description.)*
   ____ Poor
   ____ Fair
   ____ Good
   ____ Excellent

7. How successful is he at
   a. Making worthwhile plans?
      ____ Poor
      ____ Fair
      ____ Good
      ____ Excellent
   b. Carrying them out?
      ____ Poor
      ____ Fair
      ____ Good
      ____ Excellent

8. Would you tell something about the church where he is now located and the type of work he has been doing?

   _____

   _____

   _____

9. Is he cooperative with the ministry of churches within your fellowship? _____ Explain your answer.

   _____

   _____

   _____

10. What is his relationship to other churches in the community and to community activities?

_____

_____

_____

11. What type of community would he fit into best?

____ Rural

____ Town

____ City

____ College

____ Industrial

____ Suburban

____ Other (Specify) _____

12. Does he give proper attention to his
    a. Family?

       ____ Yes   ____ No

    b. Financial obligations?

       ____ Yes   ____ No

    c. Social obligations?

       ____ Yes   ____ No

13. Does he impress people as having a sincere, unselfish spirit of service? How?

_____

14. Has he any special natural gifts that add to his effectiveness? _____ Name them.

_____

_____

_____

15. What has he achieved in the church and in the community?

_____

_____

_____

Personal Qualities

(Please place a check by **one item under each of the following headings.** An explanation may be made in the right margin if you wish to support or qualify your judgment. Do not check items about which you feel uncertain or have had no opportunity to observe.)

PHYSICAL CONDITION
    ____ Frequently incapacitated
    ____ Somewhat below average
    ____ Fairly good health
    ____ Good health
    ____ Rugged and vigorous

PERSONALITY TRAITS
    ____ Avoided by others
    ____ Tolerated by others
    ____ Liked by most people
    ____ Well liked
    ____ Sought by others

INTELLIGENCE
    ____ Learns and thinks slowly
    ____ Average mental ability
    ____ Alert—has a good mind
    ____ Brilliant—exceptional capacity

JUDGMENT
    ____ Makes "snap" decisions
    ____ Finds it difficult to make any decisions
    ____ Has sound judgment and good common sense
    ____ Carefully evaluates each issue

ACHIEVEMENT/INITIATIVE
    ____ Does only what is assigned
    ____ Prone to start but does not finish
    ____ Meets average expectations
    ____ Resourceful and effective
    ____ Superior creative ability

LEADERSHIP QUALITIES
    ____ Makes no effort to be a leader
    ____ Tries to lead but lacks ability
    ____ Has some leadership promise
    ____ Good leadership ability
    ____ Unusual ability as a leader

ABILITY TO WORK WITH OTHERS
    ____ Frequently causes friction
    ____ Prefers to work alone

_____ Usually cooperative

_____ Works well with others

_____ Most effective in teamwork

RESPONSIVENESS

_____ Slow to sense how others feel

_____ Reasonably responsive

_____ Usually well-balanced

_____ Well balanced and controlled

_____ Maintains balance and control even under most difficult circumstances

WILLINGNESS TO SERVE

_____ Reluctant to serve

_____ Usually willing to serve

_____ Willing to serve but not dependable

_____ Eager to serve and very dependable

FINANCIAL RESPONSIBILITY

_____ Does not seem to know how to manage on present income

_____ Does not always spend wisely

_____ Gives the impression of being somewhat extravagant

_____ Has learned to live within his income

_____ Handles finances wisely

Please evaluate the following qualifications by checking **one** of the four categories. (*Omit items about which you feel uncertain.*)

Characteristic	Excellent	Above Average	Average	Below Average
General knowledge of the Bible				
Evidence of a life of prayer				
Genuine love for souls, leading to earnest efforts to win them for Christ				
Trustworthy and conscientious				
Patience under trial				
Energy and enterprise				
Cooperation with authorities				
Ability to make decisions				
Sense of humor				

1. Does the candidate impress you as being a Christian of developed character and mature Christian experience? _____ Explain your answer.

   _____

   _____

   _____

2. Is the candidate's home life such that it is an asset and example in Christian service and leadership? _____ Explain your answer.

_____
_____
_____
_____

3 Is the candidate's home warm toward Christian hospitality? _____ Explain your answer.

_____
_____
_____
_____

4. Does the candidate demonstrate a "shepherd's heart" (genuine concern and love for people)? _____ Explain your answer.

_____
_____
_____

5. In your judgment, does the candidate have a healthy view of God's plan for the local church? _____ Explain your answer.

_____
_____
_____

6. How would you rate the candidate's potential for an effective ministry as a pastor?

_____

7. Are there issues, positive or negative, not referred to in these sheets that you believe we should consider concerning this candidate? Please feel free to mention them frankly and fully.

_____
_____
_____
_____
_____

_____   _____
(Signature)   (Date)

Suggested Procedures and Questions for the Interview with the Candidate

Setting

A neutral location, such as a restaurant or a motel, is preferred for this interview. Make sure you have at least two to four hours with the candidate in a setting where you will not be disturbed. Because both the candidate and the committee are still in the exploratory stage, any place that would expose him to his or your church could be detrimental. It is important to establish a good rapport so that all present can be relaxed and the candidate will not feel intimidated. If your committee plans to conduct the interview via conference call, each member should know before the call which questions he/she will ask.

Process

Each committee member should know his questions for the candidate before the interview. The participation of every committee member is important. It will help the candidate address each member and establish bridges of communication. Questions need not be asked in order. The process should flow easily.

Each committee member should have the complete list of questions and should take notes on all answers. If other questions arise, monitor them carefully so that they will not take the time allotted for the prepared list of questions. You want to be able to have all questions answered satisfactorily.

It is good if you record the session, but you must inform the candidate. If you discuss a sensitive area of personal concern that the candidate does not wish recorded, you must stop the recorder during that period in the discussion.

It would be good to have the candidate's wife attend this session.

Questions during Interview

The following are questions you may wish to present to the candidate.
Many pastoral research committees ask these questions.

1. I would be interested, in three to five minutes, about when and how you became a Christian. *(If his wife is present, ask her the same question.)*
2. What happened in your life to lead you into the ministry?
3. How do you understand a call from God?
4. What has affirmed the call of God in your life during recent months? *(If his wife is present, ask her how she feels about her husband's being in the ministry.)*
5. How did you become involved in our Fellowship? *(If he has never been involved, ask, "Why have you sought placement in our church?")*
6. Our church is congregational in government. How do you interpret congregationalism?

How do *you* carry out *your* ministry and administration in congregational government?

7. Is there any point in our doctrinal statement (association [GARBC] and/or local church) that you would not or could not affirm?

   (If he answers in the affirmative, continue your questions.) Which points and why? *(It would be proper to ask about doctrines or viewpoints, if any, that are important to your church and/or have caused tension in the church. Examples are eternal security, neoevangelicalism, ecumenism, Calvinism/Arminianism, eschatology, and Pentecostalism/ charismatic movement.)*

8. Are you involved with the state and/or national Fellowship (GARBC)?

9. a. Would you briefly tell us what your home atmosphere was like (that is, your child-hood home)? *(Questions b. and c. are optional.)*

   b. What was the attitude of your parents to each other?

   c. How did this make you feel?

   (Guide to the interviewer: Ask yourself, was the family well adjusted? Is there any evidence of anxiety or emotional disturbances due to the family relationships?)

10. How does your family feel about your being in the ministry?

11. Have you ever had any difficulties with depression, moodiness, anxiety, or other similar difficulties? What was the cause? *(An affirmative answer does not disqualify him. In fact, his experience will probably make him more understanding. You may want to omit this question if you feel you do not have a good rapport with the candidate.)*

12. What do you do to maintain your health?

13. Do you become upset easily? What upsets you?

14. How do you react when things do not go as you planned?

15. How do you respond to criticism? How do you respond to criticism from someone you respect very much? How do you respond when you believe the criticism is unjustified? What have you done in such a case?

16. How do you think you relate to other people? How do you think people see you? How would you like them to see you?

17. In what areas of ministry do you feel most experienced and competent?

18. What do you think are your "non-strengths"? What makes you lack confidence in your abilities in this area/these areas?

19. How do you feel about your being in a leadership position?

20. What do you do in your spare time?

Questions on Doctrine
The committee should review the candidate's statement on doctrine and then produce at least twenty questions concerning his position. Some sample questions follow:

21. How do you define and view inerrancy in relation to the Bible?

22. What steps do you follow in leading an individual to Christ?

23. How do you view the ordinances in relation to salvation?

24. How do you view the ordinances in relation to church membership?

25. Are there any books of the Bible you would not use in preaching? Explain your answer.

26. How do you view the ministry of the Holy Spirit?

27. How do you interpret the imminent return of Christ?

28. Who should join or be a member of the church?

29. Is there a real Heaven? Is it eternal?

30. Is Hell real? Are the torments mentioned in Scripture merely symbolic? Is Hell eternal?

31. Are the unsaved lost and cast out from God forever? Why or why not?

32. What hours do you expect to spend in study without interruption, except for emergencies?

33. What is your position on tithing? on "faith promise" giving?

34. What is your attitude toward marriage of divorced people, mixed marriages (saved/unsaved), and marriage of unbelievers?

35. How do you use premarital counseling?

36. What is your attitude toward church finance, suppers, sales, and so on?

37. What do you think about cooperation with ecumenical programs?

38. What do you feel about cooperating with other churches in the community—fundamental? evangelical? liberal?

39. What is your attitude toward missions and missions giving?

40. What is the procedure of obtaining permission before accepting speaking engagements that would take you out of town?

41. What do you expect of the deacons?

42. Are you satisfied with your present education, or do you want to further your formal education?

43. What programs would you like to introduce to our church?

44. What is your view of creation?

45. What is the role of the Holy Spirit today?

46. What is the place of spiritual gifts in the church?

You will probably have other questions that are unique to your church. Ask them as well. List them here.

Questions after Interview

After this interview each committee member should answer the following questions:

1. Does this candidate have a good grasp of Scripture and a good doctrinal position that would strengthen our people in their spiritual growth?
2. Does the candidate believe doctrines that are contrary to our statement of faith?
3. Do any obvious policies disqualify the applicant? If so, state them.
4. What do you consider the main assets of this candidate?
5. What is likely to be the candidate's main difficulty or handicap with us? How can it be remedied?
6. What degree of success would you predict for the candidate if we called him to be our pastor?

_____ Poor

_____ Fair

_____ Good

_____ Very good

_____ Outstanding

Remuneration of the Pastor

Biblical Principle

"Let the elders that rule well be counted worthy of double honour, especially they who labour in the word and doctrine. For the scripture saith, Thou shalt not muzzle the ox that treadeth out the corn. And, The labourer is worthy of his reward" (1 Timothy 5:17, 18).

These verses address full-time vocational Christian service and give several principles.

1. The apostle Paul valued the ministry of the gospel of Christ when he used the term "double honour." Because of the context, "honour" has to include salary, among other things.

2. Paul was telling the church to consider a pastor's salary in comparison with those in their community who have honor. A church may not be able to pay a pastor double the salary of the "honorable" in the community, but it nevertheless should be an incentive or goal. Paul affirmed that the pastor is worthy of a double portion.

3. The view of a pastor's salary also reflects the church's view of the value of the ministry. Galatians 6:6 says, "Let him that is taught in the word communicate unto him that teacheth in all good things."

The phrase "all good things" surely includes more than material things, but it does include at least that. Certainly it requires the church to share generously with the pastor for the well-being of his life.

Philosophy of Remuneration

Often we have heard, "You keep the pastor humble, Lord, and we'll keep him poor." We need to seriously think through the philosophy of giving and remuneration in a church. The following are some practical, important considerations you must make as a pastoral search committee.

1. Compensation for the paid staff should be based on the value of the individual to the church.

2. Consideration should be given to the community and the economic level in which the pastor serves.

3. Pay should allow the pastor and/or staff to afford to live in a style with those whom they serve.

4. A consideration must be placed on the church's ability to pay. The pastor should not pay the church's mortgage or pay for the church's mission budget by taking lower compensation.

5. The church needs to allow room to grow in compensation.

6. Pay helps build the pastor's confidence.

7. Pay range needs to be established for all paid staff.

8. Benefits are a part of the total overall package and should be viewed in a similar manner to industry.
9. External factors, such as cost of living, need to be viewed.
10. The church needs to determine what type of image will be given to the congregation and community when it establishes its pay levels.
11. Compensation for associate pastors should be pegged in relation to the pastor's salary.
12. All salaries should have a range so as to reward paid staff for performance and establish the growth potential for each position.

Practical Criteria for Establishing Remuneration

1. Consideration should be given to the average level of compensation in the community.
2. Comparable positions need to be considered when establishing pay levels for church positions.
   Accountant—$_____
   Other Senior Pastors in Area—$_____
   Attorney—$_____
   Local School Principals—$_____
   Engineer—$_____
   Community's Median Wage—$_____
3. Consideration should be given to the average level of compensation in the congregation.
4. Consider the current compensation level for the individual.
5. The church board must view performance and goal accomplishment.
6. Length of service and education need to enter into the picture.
7. Take into account the number of people the person is directly supervising.
8. Note the size of the congregation.
9. Bear in mind the ability of the congregation to pay.
10. Obey the Biblical perspectives of 1 Timothy 5:17 and 18.

Benefits for the Pastor

1. Almost all employees in industry receive several supplemental or fringe benefits. These benefits help the employees reduce their taxable income.
2. Fringe benefits, such as health insurance, life insurance, automobile, FICA, and pension should be separated from the cash compensation for the paid staff.
3. Listed below are the results of the Bureau of Labor Statistics showing the percentage of workers receiving the following benefits:

Paid Vacation 99%

Holidays (average number of annual paid holidays is 10.2 days)	99%
Free Life Insurance	81%
Noncontributory Private Pension Plans	79%
Sick Leave (the average sick leave is 5–30 days)	65%
Free Health Insurance	71%
Free Health Insurance for Dependents	48%

Free Accident and Sickness Insurance	41%
Free Dental Care Insurance	24%
Free Vision Care	8%
Free Long-Term Disability Insurance	32%
Paid Personal Leave (the average is 2–5 days)	23%

Remuneration Schedule to be Considered for the Pastoral Candidate

Moving Expenses

All transportation expenses will be paid from your present home to _____. These expenses include transportation of household goods and library via a van line or method approved by yourself and the church. It also includes mileage at _____ cents per mile, for one car plus necessary meals and lodging en route for you and your family.

Salary and Benefits

The Pastor's basic salary shall be a designated amount paid every other Sunday or as agreed upon. The church board each year will designate part of this amount as a housing allowance, based upon the pastor's estimate of expenses to be incurred the next calendar year. The salary shall be reviewed at least once each year, and adjustment shall be made according to the financial growth of the church and the national economy.

• Salary: Cash Value* _____   Benefit Value** _____

• Other Benefits:

  1. Housing

     A home is provided for the dwelling of the pastor and his family, which has been estimated at a yearly rental value of _____.

  2. Housing Allowance

     This amount shall be paid the pastor as a housing allowance for owning his own home.

     _____

  3. Utilities for Pastor's Home

     This amount shall be paid for heat, electricity, water, phone (except personal long distance). _____

  4. Automobile Allowance

     This amount shall be given annually to the pastor for the use of his car in church-related business. _____

  5. Insurance and Retirement Expenses

     The following insurance programs shall be underwritten for the pastor:

     Hospitalization _____

     Retirement _____

     Total _____

*Cash Value: When money actually is paid to the pastor for his services or for pastoral ministries.
**Benefit Value: When an expense for the pastoral ministry is paid directly by the church and the pastor does not handle the money.

Schedule for the Candidate's Visit

Pastors often remark that they really did not have adequate time while they were candidating at a church. We do not know how much time is enough, but certainly a Saturday and Sunday are insufficient. It would be advisable to have the candidate and his family visit for at least four days. The travel cost will be the same. Lodging and meals will amount only to a few extra dollars, dollars that will be well spent.

The following schedule cannot be used entirely, as the candidate and his family could not physically endure all the activities. But it contains ideas to consider.

Whatever your plans, the agenda for the activities should be written out and sent to the candidate before he comes to the church.

If the candidate could arrive on Thursday afternoon, here is a possible slate of events:

Thursday evening: Have a dinner meeting with the candidate, his wife, the pulpit committee members, and their wives. The pulpit committee should be the first group to meet with the candidate.

Friday morning: Give him time to relax and make final preparations for Sunday.

Friday lunch: The candidate and family should be guests in someone's home for the noon meal.

Friday evening: The candidate could meet with each board and committee in a group dinner meeting. He could sit at the head of a semicircle, where he could be seen, and ask each of the leaders questions that would relate to the function of his/her board or committee. The chairman should then have opportunity to ask the candidate his ideas on the duties of each board or committee.

While the candidate is in this meeting, the wives of the church board and committee members could be hostessing the candidate's wife at an informal tea. Appropriate provisions should be made for the pastor's children.

Saturday morning: Allow the pastor and his family to relax.

Saturday noon: The pastor and his family should enjoy dinner in someone's home or a potluck meal at the church, open to all the church family. It could possibly be a fun time or a time for the candidate and/or his wife to tell about their family (with pictures, if possible) if the children did not accompany them.

Saturday afternoon: Someone should be delegated to give the candidate and his wife a tour of the community, area, parsonage, church, and so forth.

Saturday early evening: They should be guests at someone else's home for the evening meal. A time for questions from the congregation should be planned as part of this evening. This meeting should close early enough so that the pastor can return to his accommodations for adequate rest for Sunday.

Sunday morning: The candidate should meet with the combined adult Sunday School classes. The candidate could share his testimony, conversion, call, training, personal goals. His wife could also share her testimony and relationship to the local church as the pastor's wife. Or the candidate could visit the Sunday School departments or teach a class.

Worship service: The service should be a normal service. The preliminaries/worship could be handled by a church leader or the candidate. The candidate will obviously be the speaker.

Sunday noon: Candidate and family are guests in someone's home for dinner.

Sunday afternoon: This is a time for relaxation and final preparation for Sunday evening.

Sunday evening: Candidate could be a guest in someone's home for a light meal before the evening service.

Youth meetings: Candidate could observe your youth meeting if it is held on Sunday evenings, or he should meet informally with the youth.

Evening service: The candidate could be in charge of the entire service, or this time could be used for questions and answers (see Saturday early evening).

After the **evening service:** Hold either a coffee reception or a final meeting with the pulpit committee. If a coffee reception is held, the pulpit committee members should have a few minutes with the candidate for final questions from him and to him.

Someone should be designated to take the candidate to the airport if he traveled by air. Also, if the pastor has come by air, provide a vehicle for him during his stay.

*(**NOTE:** The candidate's wife should be with him at meals and informal times. At board and committee meetings, it is best if she is not present. You are calling a pastor, not his wife.*

Do not schedule the candidate to eat at the same home more than once. Let several families have the opportunity to get acquainted in that way.

At least three weeks prior to his coming, prepare a handout and/or a bulletin board giving pertinent information concerning the candidate. This exposure will give the congregation an opportunity to acquaint themselves with him even before he arrives. A picture of his family should also be included.)

Sample Call Letter

The letter of call should be concise and should include all pertinent information. It is a type of contract. This list may need to be added to, deleted from, or changed to fit your local situation. The following is a sample.

Rev. _____
0000 Any Street
Somewhere, U.S.A.

Dear _____:

With gratitude to God, I have the pleasure to inform you that by a _____ positive and _____ negative vote, the members of the _____ Church of _____, on _____ (*date*) extend to you a call to become their pastor.
The church members enthusiastically accepted the pulpit committee's recommendation and thanked God for the unity directed by the Holy Spirit. We hope that your response will be the same.
The terms of the call are as follows:
The church will provide

1. An annual cash salary of _____.
2. A parsonage for your use or a housing allowance of _____ per year.
3. A utilities allowance of _____ per year.
4. An annual automobile expense allowance of _____.
5. An annual payment of _____ toward a retirement plan.
6. Full payment of premiums for family health and hospital coverage.
7. Expenses of attending the annual conference [GARBC] and state Association meetings.
8. _____ weeks of paid vacation per year.
9. At least one week's study leave each year with $_____ being allowed annually toward this ongoing education.
10. _____ Sundays annually for you to be away as a speaker, with the church paying the pulpit supply. Arrangement for your absence must be cleared with our _____ board.

(*continued on page 90*)

_____
89

11. Your moving expense from your present residence to
_____, which will include _____ cents per mile
for one car, meals, and lodging for you and your family en route to
_____ during the move.

These above items will be reviewed annually by the budget committee.
We understand that as our pastor-elect, if you accept the call, you agree:
1. To accept the pastoral leadership of the
_____ Church of
_____, _____ (date).
You may wish to include a list of pastoral expectations. This could be
a type of job description. See Items N and T.

2. To accept the by-laws and constitution of the _____ Church,
to prayerfully seek guidance from the leaders of the church, and to
work in harmony with them.

We have endeavored to carefully and implicitly outline the arrangement
in this call. If, however, you desire further information, please phone me
collect at _____.
We join you in prayer as you consider this call, and we await your written reply within the next two weeks.

By order of the church,

Chairman or Secretary
Pulpit Committee

Suggested Expectations for a Pastor

A church often fails to take time to determine the details of its pastor's job. As a result, the pastor may not be sure he is doing what the people expect. Also, the congregation may wonder why their pastor is doing what he is doing (or not doing what he is not doing). The following guidelines can be tailored to fit your church's expectations for a pastor.

Title

Pastor _____ Church of _____

Purpose

The pastor, as God's appointed shepherd to the church in _____, has as his first responsibility a personal relationship to God as outlined in Romans 12:1 and 2. As a man of God, his second responsibility is to his family. As shepherd to the church, he shall devote his time to the work of the church, administration of the ordinances, and the preaching of the Word. He shall, with great patience, be ready to reprove, rebuke, and exhort to maintain spiritual unity, and to rightly divide the Word of Truth (1 Timothy 3:1–7; 4:12–15; 2 Timothy 2:15; Titus 1:7–9).

He shall be in agreement with the stated objectives of the church and shall uphold its constitution.

Responsibilities

1. The pastor shall provide a pulpit ministry that incorporates the exposition of Scriptures in all doctrine, presentation of a clear message of salvation, and exhortation of the church constituency to act upon Scriptural teaching in their daily lives (2 Timothy 2:2).
2. The pastor shall spend much time in prayer and personal Bible study so that he may experience spiritual growth and educational development in his personal life and ministry. He shall set regular study hours during which he shall not be disturbed, except for emergencies.
3. The pastor shall be responsible for administering the ordinances of baptism and communion at the regularly scheduled and special services.
4. The pastor shall be available for personal counseling of the members and friends of the church.
5. The pastor shall instruct, train, and encourage; shall participate in church; and shall regularly visit the sick and aged.
6. The pastor shall perform his duties as set forth in the constitution, through the delegation of these responsibilities to its various lay leaders and church staff (*fill in according to your local constitution and by-laws*). Furthermore, he shall coordinate the staff and lay leaders in such a manner that he encourages their participation in the regular services of the church.

7. The pastor shall be responsible for holding an instruction class for prospective members covering with them the Confession of Faith as set forth in the constitution, the organization of the church, and any other areas related to the Christian life and the church.
8. The pastor shall be responsible for holding an instruction class for prospective members covering with them the Confession of Faith as set forth in Article _____ of the Constitution, the organization of the church and any other areas related to the Christian life and the church.
9. The pastor is encouraged to attend annual conferences (GARBC) and be free to accept leadership roles in the Fellowship and the state association, providing such activities do not hinder his ministry to this congregation.

Relationships

1. The pastor shall supervise all paid staff of the church.
2. The pastor shall cooperate with the trustees in their supervision of the church custodian.
3. The pastor, as a member of the various church boards and committees, shall be responsible for their spiritual leadership.
4. The pastor shall be responsible for the spiritual leadership of the congregation, but he is responsible to the congregation for his administrative function through the church boards.

Other Areas

"Other areas" reflects particular needs presently felt in your church. Some examples are as follow:

1. Develop growth groups.
2. Visit all members of the church once a year.
3. Develop evangelistic visitation.

NOTE: This list is only a suggestion. It may be altered in any way necessary for the committee to fit the local needs. Make sure it is not long and that it allows flexibility. This list of expectations should be reviewed, evaluated, and revised as needed. Pastors and churches are neither mechanical in function nor stagnant.

Sample Installation Service

Scheduling

The installation service is the formal recognition by the church of its new pastor. Usually two to three months pass between the time the pastor accepts the call and when he actually arrives at the church. All the preparations can be made during this period.

1. Set a date so that the state representative (GARBC), any special guests of the pastor, and area dignitaries (such as the town mayor) can make plans to attend.
2. Many installation services are held during the regular Sunday morning worship service so that more of the constituents can attend.
3. The service is followed by a reception, which may be either a meal or just "coffee." The kind of reception depends on the time of the service and the facilities of the church.

Order of Service

1. Prelude
2. Call to Worship (defining purpose of the service)
3. Invocation (conducted by the church board chairman)
4. Hymn
5. Greetings *(Limit to three minutes; read portions of any letters of greeting received.)*
6. Special music
7. Message (Given by a special friend of the pastor or a leader in the state or national Fellowship; twenty minutes in length.)
8. Hymn
9. Charge to congregation (Given by a special friend of the pastor or a leader in the state or national Fellowship; eight minutes in length.)
10. Response (Given by the church chairman; two minutes in length.)
11. Charge to pastor (Given by a special friend of the pastor or a leader in the state or national Fellowship; twenty minutes in length.)
12. Prayer of installation *(The church deacons or the members of the board are asked to come forward to stand in a semicircle around the pastor during prayer. The pastor should kneel facing the congregation, with his wife standing at his side. The prayer can be offered by a church board member.)*
13. Response by pastor (three minutes in length)
14. Hymn
15. Benediction (pastor)

Miscellaneous Letters to Be Sent

The following list includes letters that are not listed in the item index but that must be sent out by the pastoral search committee. To clarify the list, here is a review of the steps with which these letters relate:

1. Acquire names and résumés
2. Review all potential candidates
3. Verify responses
4. Screen possible candidates
5. Evaluate the candidate
6. Evaluate the candidate's preaching performance
7. Choose several prime candidates
8. Select one prime candidate
9. Discuss the church board's support and the pastor's remuneration
10. Vote on and call the candidate as pastor

Step	To Whom	Reason
1		
2		
3	Those who replied positively	To thank them for being potential candidates
3	Those who replied negatively	To thank them for their reply and consideration
4	Unacceptable candidate	To thank him for being a potential candidate and to explain that he did not fulfill the church profile
5	Unacceptable candidate	To thank him for being a potential candidate and to explain that he does not fit the church's profile
6		
7	Unacceptable candidate	To thank him for being a potential candidate and to explain that he does not fit the church's profile
8		
9	Candidate	To thank him, to set the date of candidating, and to send a schedule (Item L, p. 87)
10	Other candidate still held as a potential in Step 8	To thank him for being a candidate and to inform him of the call of a new pastor

Candidate Evaluation Worksheet

Committee member's name _____

The Candidate Evaluation Worksheet is designed to help the committee more quickly evaluate the response from the whole committee. This evaluator is designed so that each committee member must have his/her own sheet.

The **quantitative** and **subjective** categories from your pastoral profile should be listed in the columns on the left as indicated. The names of the candidates should be listed in the top spaces of the right-hand column *(note example on page 100)*.

After the evaluation sheets are complete, enter the totals of the **quantitative** and **subjective** values on the Cumulative Candidate Worksheets (Items Q2 and Q3, pp. 98, 99).

Quantitative	Subjective
True—1	Below average— -1 (minus one)
Not true—0	Average—1
	Above average—2

Potential Candidate

Total Quantitative Criteria							
Total Subjective Criteria							
Total Quantitative and Subjective Criteria							

Cumulative Candidate Worksheet— Quantitative

(See sample on page 101.) After each committee member has finished filling out his Candidate Evaluation Worksheet (Item Q1, p. 97), the information should be recorded on the grid below:

QUANTITATIVE TOTALS	Candidates' Names and Quantitative Totals						
Names of Committee Members							
Total Quantitative Criteria							
Average Quantitative Criteria							

(For average, take each total and divide it by the number of committee members.)

Cumulative Candidate Worksheet— Subjective

(See sample on page 102.) After each committee member has finished filling out his Candidate Evaluation Worksheet (Item Q1, p. 97), the information should be recorded on the grid below:

SUBJECTIVE TOTALS	Candidates' Names and Subjective Totals					
Names of Committee Members						
Total Subjective Criteria						
Average Subjective Criteria						

(For average, take each total and divide it by the number of committee members.)

When the average totals have been completed, place each candidate's information on the Pastoral Candidate Ranking Graph (Item R1, p. 103). After you have completed this exercise, you will see clearly which are your high- and low-potential candidates.

Candidate Evaluation Sample

Committee member's name _____**Martha Peterson**_____

The Candidate Evaluation Worksheet is designed to help the committee more quickly evaluate the response from the whole committee. This evaluator is designed so that each committee member must have his/her own sheet.

The **quantitative** and **subjective** categories from your pastoral profile should be listed in the columns on the left as indicated. The names of the candidates should be listed in the top spaces of the right-hand column (*note example below*).

After the evaluation sheets are complete, enter the totals of the **quantitative** and **subjective** values on the Cumulative Candidate Worksheets (Items Q2 and Q3, pp. 98, 99).

Quantitative	**Subjective**	Plum	Gonzales	Madison	Jones	Smith	Peterson	
True—1	Below average— -1 (minus one)							
Not true—0	Average—1 Above average—2							
Potential Candidate								
Seminary graduate		1	1	1	0	1	0	
Orthodox/evangelical background		1	1	1	1	1	1	
Married		1	1	1	1	1	1	
Accepts statement of faith		1	1	1	1	0	1	
Five years experience		0	0	1	0	1	1	
Accepts our church's constitution		1	0	0	1	1	1	
Bilingual?		0	1	1	0	1	1	
Total Quantitative Criteria		5	5	6	4	6	6	
A people/relational person		1	2	1	1	1	1	
Good pulpit ministry		2	1	1	1	-1	2	
Good with senior citizens		2	2	-1	-1	1	1	
Motivates people		1	1	-1	-1	1	1	
Shows love to people		1	1	-1	2	1	1	
Seems hospitable		1	1	1	1	2	1	
Total Subjective Criteria		8	8	0	6	5	7	
Total Quantitative and Subjective Criteria		13	13	6	10	11	13	

Cumulative Candidate Sample— Quantitative

After each committee member has finished filling out his Candidate Evaluation Worksheet (Item Q1, p. 97), the information should be recorded on the grid below:

QUANTITATIVE TOTALS

Names of Committee Members	Plum	Gonzales	Madison	Jones	Smith	Peterson	
Martha Peterson	5	5	6	4	6	6	
Sven Olson	4	5	6	7	2	2	
Elizar Oretz	6	7	5	5	2	2	
Carl Ekstein	4	6	7	5	2	3	
Neal Smith	7	7	7	7	2	2	
Total Quantitative Criteria	26	30	31	28	14	15	
Average Quantitative Criteria	5.2	6	6.2	5.6	2.8	3	

Candidates' Names and Quantitative Totals

(For average, take each total and divide it by the number of committee members.)

Cumulative Candidate Sample— Subjective

After each committee member has finished filling out his Candidate Evaluation Worksheet (Item Q1, p. 97), the information should be recorded on the grid below:

SUBJECTIVE TOTALS						
Names of Committee Members	Plum	Gonzales	Madison	Jones	Smith	Peterson
Martha Peterson	8	8	0	6	5	7
Sven Olson	8	9	6	6	10	6
Elizar Oretz	9	11	7	6	11	3
Carl Ekstein	10	10	3	6	6	2
Neal Smith	9	9	9	9	9	2
Total Subjective Criteria	44	47	25	33	41	20
Average Subjective Criteria	8.9	9.4	5	6.6	8.2	4

Candidates' Names and Subjective Totals

(For average, take each total and divide it by the number of committee members.)

When the average totals have been completed, place each candidate's information on the Pastoral Candidate Ranking Graph (Item R1, p. 103). After you have completed this exercise, you will see clearly which are your high- and low-potential candidates.

Pastoral Candidate Ranking Graph

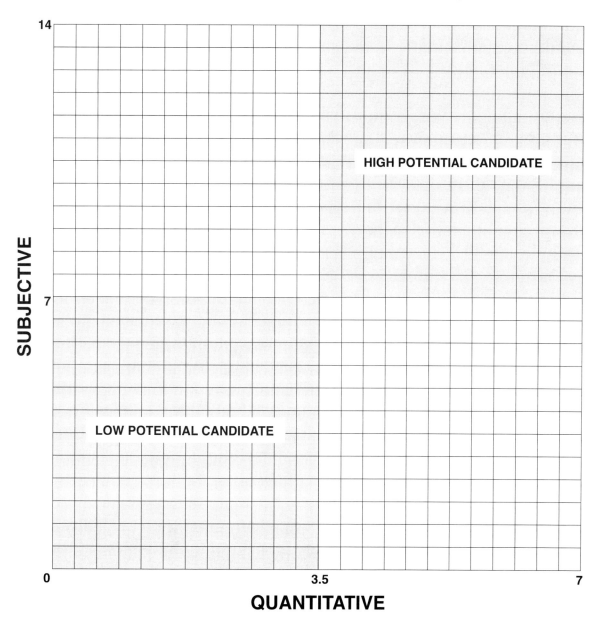

Pastoral Candidate Ranking Sample

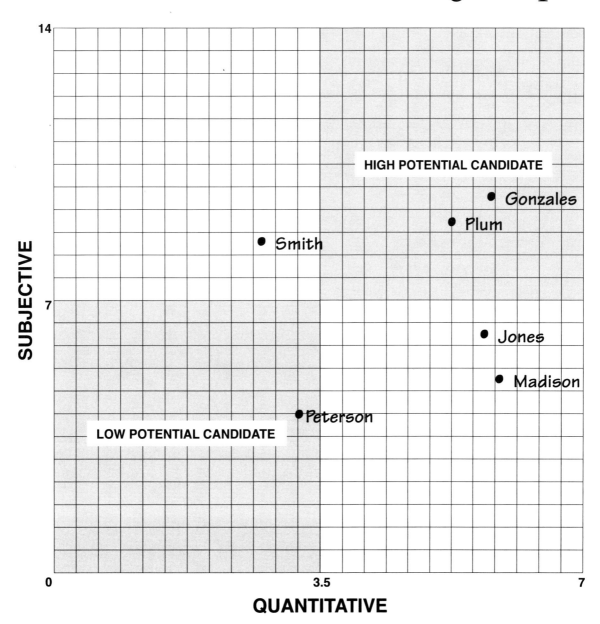

Pastoral Candidate Ranking Explanation

In looking at the sample, you can quickly extract several obvious pieces of information.

1. There was a difference of opinion both in the subjective and quantitative responses.

2. Rev. Gonzales and Rev. Plum are high-potential candidates.

3. Rev. Peterson is a low-potential candidate.

4. Rev. Jones and Rev. Madison fit the quantitative criteria well, but did not make a strong subjective impression on the committee. They were qualified, but just did not make the committee feel good about them.

5. Rev. Smith, although he did not fit the quantitative criteria, made a good impression on the committee. It is helpful to view these results on the chart, as people will often make decisions based on how they feel rather than on the realities. Such decisions can be dangerous for the church's future. If the committee wants to consider this man, they must review his résumé and the ways in which he did not fill the quantitative issues.

Candidate Follow-up Information

Name _____

Church/Position _____

_____

Address _____
      (Street)   (City)   (State or Province)   (Zip Code or Postal Code)   (Country)

Work phone _____

Home phone _____

E-mail _____

Fax _____

Comments _____

Submitted by _____

Heard by _____

_____ Rejected

_____ Tabled

_____ Further action: _____

Letter date _____

Contact by _____

Comment _____

Letter reply _____

Comments _____

_____

_____

Package sent _____

Tape requested _____

Tape received _____

Tape distributed _____

References solicited _____

_____

_____

Reference replies _____

_____

_____

Visited by_____, _____, _____,

_____, _____, _____,

_____

Thank you sent _____

Regret sent _____

Invitation sent _____

Invitation accepted _____

Coming (date) _____

Arrival (time) _____

Leaving (date) _____

Departure (time)· _____

Other comments:

_____

_____

_____

_____

_____

Pastor's Job Description— Expectations

It is not easy to write a generic job description for a senior pastor, whether as a solo pastor or as the leading member of a larger staff. However, some obvious requirements define the responsibilities of the position. On the other hand, some local church expectations, cultural norms, and/or community involvements color a pastor's tasks.

Here is another place where you will greatly use your pastoral profile. Another issue that few churches consider is how the process of activities and responsibilities changes as a church grows or a community changes.

That a pastor's job description (expectation) is not simply related to his training, competence, or abilities is an interesting and intriguing issue, especially concerning a senior pastor. His identity in the inner man is vital and is directly related to his work and his achievements in the workplace. Therefore along with the issue of the job description is the issue of personal qualifications, such as living in accordance to the Word of God (1 Timothy 3:1–7; 1 Timothy 4:12, 13; 2 Timothy 2:15; Titus 1:6–9). He must have a personal, vital, and growing relationship with Jesus Christ. He also must be confident of his call by God to the ministry. He needs to be able to relate to people and to develop good interpersonal relationships.

A church should develop a job description for its pastor for a number of reasons. One is so that he will have some clear direction as to what the church members expect of him and his time. This need may seem obvious, but many a pastor has burned out because he did not know or understand those unstated expectations. He knew he was to preach and administer, but the parishioners had an unlisted number of expectations. When the members of the congregation have unmet expectations, it is easy to become frustrated, to build straw men, and to misread the pastor's actions.

A second reason is so that when the board and pastor sit down to evaluate the past year or some events, they will have a standard by which they can evaluate the activities and action. This brings a more proper perspective and does away with irrelevant or spurious judgments by either the pastor or the board.

The following are a list of some possible expectations to place in a job description for a pastor.

1. Expected hours to work and hours in the office. Regular office hours should be published with the understanding that unexpected emergencies can arise. A pastor is on call twenty-four hours a day; therefore, he may not always be available in his office. Most pastors put in sixty hours a week or more. The church should expect that at least twenty hours are given to him for undisturbed study. Other expectations of hours need to be listed, but allow for some flexibility.

2. The job description should include the expectations of his days off, vacation, sabbaticals, and personal days. The church that encourages these times away from the church and with family will find that the pastor will better serve them when he is there.
3. Preaching and teaching
4. Visitation of constituents (members and/or attenders)
5. Discipling of leadership
6. Modeling personal evangelism
7. Administration of the ministries and staff of the church
8. Involvement in community issues
9. Special events in the church (marriages, funerals, anniversaries)
10. Education in the church (type and degree)
11. Credentials such as ordination (with whom it is carried and to whom is he responsible for the credential)
12. Experience
13. Skills, planning, organization, administration, delegation
14. Worship ministry
15. Promotion of world missions
16. Promoting personal evangelism
17. Being an active shepherd caring for the needs of the flock
18. Counseling
19. Giving quarterly and annual reports to the church. (This reporting can be very detailed as to services, visitation, and so forth, or it can be an overview of the state of the church.)
20. Participation in events, boards, and committees of the state or national association [GARBC]
21. Persons to whom he is responsible (e.g., to the congregation through the board)
22. Being ex-officio member of boards and committees. *(Spell out whether he will be a voting member or not.)*
23. Voting (On which, if any, boards will he be a voting member: general board? deacon board?)
24. Personal education (Should he be encouraged to participate in continuing education?)

As you notice, the list is very long, but it does not include the unique expectations of your local church. Therefore, a church needs to carefully and prayerfully spell out its expectations so as not to weaken the pastor's time and responsibilities to his family. Also, when the church responsibilities grow too great, it is possible for the pastor's passion for ministry to lessen and for him to suffer burnout or even to become depressed.